The Unwanted Undead Adventurer [5] Yu Okano / Illustrator: Jaian

Fairy Tale:
The Westbound Traveler

fifth

5] The Unwanted Undead Adventurer

Yu Okano
Illustrator: Jaian

Clope

Proprietor of the Three-Pronged Harpoon. Produces special weapons and armor that match Rentt's requirements.

Isabel Cariello

Loris's wife. Runs the Red Wyvern Pavilion with him. Business is good.

Loris Cariello

Proprietor of the Red Wyvern Pavilion, a tavern and eatery. Because he was saved by Rentt in the labyrinth, Rentt dines in his tavern for free.

Myullias Raiza

A Saint of the Church of Lobelia. Blessed by the spirits, she is capable of channeling divinity. Wields the powers of healing and purification.

Nive Maris

A Gold-class adventurer, as well as a vampire hunter. She is seen by many as the closest individual to Platinum-class.

Luka

Clope's Wife. Assists him in the daily operations of the Three-Pronged Harpoon.

Story

The Thousand-Year Bronze-class adventurer, Rentt, finds himself becoming an undead after being consumed by a mythical dragon. Evolving into a thrall, he manages to sneak back into the town with the aid of Rina Rupaage, a budding adventurer. Now hiding out in Lorraine's abode, he changes his name before once again setting off on the path of becoming a Mithril-class adventurer. Now having evolved into a lesser vampire, Rentt sets off to the New Moon Dungeon in search of materials, all for the sake of crafting a weapon for his disciple, Alize.

Meanwhile, a Saint from the Church of Lobelia and a Gold-class vampire hunter find themselves visiting Maalt around the same time...

Characters

Sheila Ibarss

Receptionist at the adventurer's guild. Knows Rentt's secret.

Lorraine Vivie

Scholar and Silver-class adventurer. Has been offering her support to Rentt ever since he became an undead.

Rentt Faina

An adventurer aspiring to reach Mithril-class. Became an undead after he was consumed by a dragon in the labyrinth.

Edel

A monster commonly referred to as a puchi suri. Became Rentt's familiar after sucking his blood in the basement of Maalt's Second Orphanage.

Alize

A young girl living at the orphanage. Dreams of becoming an adventurer. Currently Lorraine and Rentt's disciple.

Rina Rupaage

A new adventurer who helped Rentt sneak into Maalt after he had evolved into a ghoul.

Idoles Rouge

A knight belonging to the First Brigade of the Kingdom of Yaaran. Has a younger sister by the name of Rina.

Isaac Hart

A servant of the Latuule family. Is capable enough to take on the Tarasque Swamp on his own.

Laura Latuule

The current head of the Latuule family. Loves collecting magical items of all kinds. Rentt is contracted to periodically deliver Dragon Blood Blossoms to her from the swamp.

THE UNWANTED UNDEAD ADVENTURER: VOLUME 5
By Yu Okano

Translated by Noah Rozenberg
Edited by Suzanne Seals
English Print Cover by Mitach

Copyright © 2019 Yu Okano
Illustrations by Jaian
Cover Illustration by Jaian

First published in Japan in 2019 by OVERLAP Inc., Tokyo.
Publication rights for this English edition arranged through OVERLAP Inc., Tokyo.

Find more books like this one at www.j-novel.club!

Managing Director: Samuel Pinansky
Light Novel Line Manager: Chi Tran
Managing Editor: Jan Mitsuko Cash
Managing Translator: Kristi Fernandez
QA Manager: Hannah N. Carter
Marketing Manager: Stephanie Hii
Project Manager: Kristine Johnson

ISBN: 978-1-7183-5744-0
Printed in Korea
First Printing: April 2022
10 9 8 7 6 5 4 3 2 1

[C O N T E N T S]

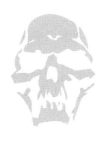

Chapter 1:   Off to Adventure

I never knew one woman could own so many books.

I had seen the extent of the Latuule family's wealth many times, but I was impressed yet again when I saw their collection of tomes. Lorraine owned tons of books too, but her library paled in comparison to the scale of this one. She also focused on her fields of study, whereas the Latuule family appeared to have works from all genres.

"It took years to build up this collection. Given enough time, it's not especially hard, actually," Laura said.

Isaac searched for anything about divinity that might help me, leaving Laura and me with our hands free. I watched the butler comb through the bookshelves and climb ladders until I began to feel guilty. It was for my sake he foraged this library. I should have helped him, but I had no clue what books were where.

Isaac seemed to have the layout committed to memory, judging by the decisive way he explored the halls. It wasn't too much trouble for him; the massive collection only meant it would take some time.

He piled up more books than I could count on the table. I questioned whether they were all necessary. Not that I hated reading, but I was in many ways a normal adventurer. I could read to an extent, including somewhat complicated texts, but technical books were sometimes difficult. I would have to rely on Lorraine for this.

"Books never go down in price, do they? I doubt I could ever buy this many."

"Really, Rentt? I've heard word about your recent accomplishments. Even putting my request aside, I heard you made plenty of money selling Tarasque parts."

It was true my sources of income had grown plentiful. I had managed to sell my Tarasque parts the other day, and while Laura's Dragon Blood Blossom request wasn't the reason for my visit, I decided I had to at least make one delivery before my trip. I'd brought some along with me and had received the reward for them earlier.

Nive's presence in town compelled me to leave Maalt as soon as I could, but long journeys required preparation. I expected it to take around a week, so I planned to stop by the Tarasque Swamp again and come back to make one more delivery. My previous venture gave me some grasp on the terrain, and I could safely enter poisonous swamps anyway. I could reach the Dragon Blood Blossoms far faster than before, so harvesting some while my preparations were underway would be more than possible.

Also, between Orcs and other monsters, I was able to collect more types of dungeon materials than ever before too. It was more than enough to live on.

But books were still inaccessible. Of course, I could afford a few books, but nothing compared to the number on display here. It would cost thousands of platinum coins, if not tens of thousands. When it came to prices that large, they were better thought of in terms of mithril coins. But I had never seen one of those. They were exclusively traded by governments and large businesses; civilians would never lay eyes on them. I imagined Laura possessed an awe-inspiring amount though.

All that aside, I had to wonder about something.

"Word travels fast, apparently. I just sold my Tarasque parts recently."

Laura smiled. "Everything that happens in Maalt reaches the Latuule family's ears."

Her response was a bit frightening to consider. I didn't know how true it was, but her family did have great influence over Maalt's operations. Maybe it wasn't that surprising that they knew about even the smallest exchanges between a man and a business.

Isaac interjected, "I believe this should do it." He finished his run through the library and stood next to a pile of tomes. Rather than stacking them all in one place, he had divided them into three categories.

Isaac gestured toward one of the stacks. "These are about the application of divinity, such as holy magic, divine magic, or holy swordsmanship. I would suggest starting with these."

The categories of divinity must have included divine and holy magic. Holy swordsmanship was the use of holy equipment as a catalyst for utilizing divinity, I assumed. I didn't know much on the subject though. When it came to divinity, I had only the barest details. Even if I wanted that knowledge, most of it was hidden from the public. The only option I had was to learn for myself.

Isaac pointed to the second stack and continued. "These texts are about divine spirits, the source of divinity. I'm sure you know how they say there are too many divine spirits to count, so these aren't comprehensive. However, they not only feature descriptions of divine spirits but also numerous records of how they came to be, so deciphering it all may take a fair bit of time and knowledge. I recommend you take it slow with these."

Many complex questions surrounded divine spirits. Most of the world's plethora of religions worshiped different deities. Even those with the same gods had different legends. There was a long history of wars between faiths that led to the demise of religions and the gods they revered on more than a few occasions. Proper research on that topic would require a vast amount of education.

I had no such education, so I would have to depend on Lorraine. I hated to ask so much of her, but she loved research anyway. The chance to read some new books would probably make her happy. But I knew I should be thankful. I appreciated all she did for me physically and mentally.

"These final texts are about your next destination, the village of Hathara. They contain folklore from around those parts. There aren't many books on the subject, but I believe they may be of some use."

The last stack Isaac mentioned was smaller than the other two. It wasn't much of a stack at all, really; there were only two books. Even so, I was shocked to learn that any texts about their local folktales even existed. Every town had some folklore, but there was seldom someone peculiar enough to try and assemble it all in written form. It would have made more sense if there were no books of the sort. And yet there were two of them.

I flipped through the pages of both books. One was a picture book, while the other was writings on folklore from all around Maalt, not just Hathara. Now I understood why these existed. Even the picture book depicted famous stories from Maalt and the surrounding area. In my youth, I had heard some of these stories from the village elder. They invoked a sense of nostalgia.

"This is plenty. I'm sure these will help me find some sort of clue. Reading them all looks like it'll take a while, but I have a friend who'll enjoy that."

"By which you mean Lorraine?" Laura asked.

She acted like there was no reason she wouldn't know that. It was somewhat startling, but it was something I had to accept.

"Yes. Right. This heap of books should delight her."

The library was full of titles I'd never seen before. The shelves at either end of the room had books you could pick up at any bookstore in Maalt, but those books were only a fraction of the full collection. The other shelves were packed with books I had never seen at a bookstore, or even at Lorraine's house. If Lorraine were here, she would most likely treat it like a treasure trove. That was all I could imagine when I commented on her.

"In that case, you're free to come here with Lorraine next time. I haven't used this room much as of late. I'm sure the books would love for someone to come read them," Laura replied.

"You wouldn't mind? Lorraine could spend the whole day here. She might even refuse to leave."

Lorraine had some common sense and knew her manners, but when she saw a book that interested her, it could cause some screws to come loose. However, if she found out I said that, she might throw a fit and insist she's not that bad.

My warning didn't faze Laura. "That's okay. She can come and go as she pleases. I've been wanting a friend who I can chat with over tea," she said.

A friend? I wondered if Laura might be lonely. It was a rude thought to have about a client, but the head of such an illustrious family might have trouble finding companionship. I found it easy to imagine. But perhaps it was only an excuse. Maybe she only said it to be considerate.

"Then I'll tell Lorraine about it next time I see her. But just in case, I'll ask again. Are you absolutely sure?" I wanted one last confirmation.

Laura nodded. "Yes, absolutely," she answered with amusement.

I left the Latuule house, joined Lorraine at her home, and went with her to the orphanage.

"By the way, Laura Latuule says I can bring you with me next time," I informed Lorraine on the way there.

She looked stunned. "Really? Everything you've told me about her made me think she's a powerful but reclusive woman."

Lorraine knew nearly everything there was to know about the families that ran this city, but the Latuule family seemed to be the sole gap in her knowledge. Their history, temperament, and ideas could only be judged by hearsay from what I told her.

I had tried to investigate them myself, but I had learned nothing. Maybe the Latuule family was powerful enough to conceal the facts, or maybe there was little to investigate to begin with. The latter seemed unlikely, though, after seeing their house, its owner, and Isaac.

The more I thought about it, the odder the family came across. But I found them awfully kind. Was that not enough? No? Of course it wasn't. But I didn't feel cautious around them. My experience thus far had been favorable deals, delightful gifts, and even assistance finding information for my own personal affairs. They were nothing but good to me.

I sometimes wondered if they had an ulterior motive. They must have, to be honest. I was doing the best I could, but I was still a lowly Bronze-class adventurer. My monstrous abilities and power over mana, spirit, and divinity all at once made me a rare specimen, but in terms of pure strength, I would barely pass for a Silver-class, at best. There was no shortage of adventurers like me out there. This family didn't need to waste its time with me.

My only guess was that they had the same goal as Nive and wanted to capture a Vampire. But in that case, they could have already done that. While I had never witnessed Isaac's power myself, a human who could tackle the Tarasque Swamp by himself had to be talented. If we ever fought, I had to assume I would lose. And knowing the size of the Latuule family's fortune, Isaac couldn't be the only one fighting for them. They could imprison me with little trouble.

I also considered that they might have had some motive for letting me act freely under their watch, but what could it be? They had nothing to gain. I was unique, but all I did was go to dungeons, hunt monsters, and make deliveries. Sometimes I roamed around night after night. If even I could accomplish their goal, it had to be faster for them to do it themselves.

Therefore, I didn't think they had a secret motive.

Probably not, at least.

In which case Laura chose to be kind to me because it was hard to find anyone who could go to the Tarasque Swamp, like she said. It was a simple, understandable, ordinary objective. Her generosity didn't seem to be fueled by any perception that I was that valuable, either. She was a wonderful person.

Yeah.

"I wouldn't say she's reclusive so much as she lives a quiet life. She doesn't draw attention to herself, but it doesn't seem to me that she's hiding away," I replied to Lorraine.

She looked conflicted. "Then why can I hardly find anything when I try to research her?"

"Hardly? As in you found more than nothing?"

"Yes. I found her family name in some old notes for city council meetings. It looks like her family's actually involved in running the city. But they haven't done much of anything recently. And by recently, I mean in the last century."

"That's some impressive research."

The council meetings were led by the local lord and involved many of Maalt's influential families in deciding how the city should be run. The meeting notes wouldn't be shown to a civilian. But somehow, Lorraine had managed to read them.

"I got some help. They asked me to pay them back by making a little medicine, but that's not a big deal."

It was an exchange, in other words. The medicine Lorraine made with alchemy was highly effective. She must have been asked for help from an acquaintance who knew as much.

Lorraine possessed plenty of skill, but she only sold the most common goods to Maalt's drug stores and adventurer's guilds. The sole way to acquire special medicine from her was to negotiate, but she put her research first. Lorraine often turned down requests; it was only at times like these she would accept them.

"Your craft can certainly come in handy sometimes. I should have studied alchemy." Then maybe back when I was an ordinary Bronze-class adventurer, I wouldn't have been so poor. It made sense in the moment, but Lorraine shook her head.

"I'm sure you could learn alchemy now, but you certainly didn't have enough mana for it before. I doubt it would've been possible," she declared.

Well, I was more than aware of that at the time. That was why I never learned it, despite knowing a master alchemist.

Alchemy wasn't impossible without mana, but if you wanted to profit off it, you needed a certain amount. You could use mana stones to supplement your mana each time, but the cost and time investment would get increasingly steep. If it came to that, hunting monsters and making deliveries was more efficient.

"So, why's Laura inviting me anyway?"

Lorraine got back on topic, so I answered her. "Well, last time I visited the Latuule house, I told them I was off to investigate the source of my divinity, some divine spirit that had blessed me. They lent me some documents to help out."

"Oh really? As in books? That's outside my field of study, so I wouldn't have too much on that subject."

Lorraine did have some relevant research, but only what was commonly available. She had nothing that revealed the Church's secrets. The books I borrowed from Laura, however, appeared at a glance to feature loads of information not meant for the public. I had to wonder why she had those. It was a mystery, but there was no use thinking about it.

At any rate, I told Lorraine more. "Yes, books. And they kept them in an incredible library. It was an enormous room with bookshelves from wall to wall. Even the walls were bookshelves stuffed with tomes from ceiling to floor. All their books looked valuable."

Lorraine's face brightened. "What?! Is that what she's inviting me for?!"

"Right. I told her I'm friends with a bookworm that I'd love to show the place, then Laura said she knew I was talking about you and you're free to come any time."

"Nice work, Rentt. I'm happy enough to lick your boots if you ask now."

She didn't look like she was joking, so I thought it was best to decline.

Then Lorraine calmed down and spoke again. "So you only mentioned me as your friend, but she knew you meant me? When you think about it, that's kind of frightening. You never told her about me, did you?"

"I didn't, no."

This was peculiar, but it indicated Laura had considerable skill at gathering information. This family's interest in me remained bizarre, however. Maybe Lorraine thought so too.

"Well, if they're letting me borrow books, then I'm sure they're a wonderful family. But relaxing too much around them sounds like a bad idea," she said.

But Lorraine still decided to go visit the Latuule house. The promise of books had her captivated.

Lorraine and I stood outside the door to the orphanage and faced each other. We were deciding who should knock.

"Go ahead," I suggested.

"No, you can do it," Lorraine responded.

We glared at each other for a while, but I was stubborn enough that Lorraine gave in. "Fine, then." She touched the knocker and tapped it on the door. As expected, there was a loud snap as the knocker broke off the door.

"I knew it. That's why I didn't want to."

Lorraine sighed and looked at me, but I had already taken out a powerful slime adhesive.

"Nice to see you were prepared," Lorraine muttered and reached out for the adhesive, but we were in for a surprise that day.

"Hello? Who is it?"

Before we could paste the knocker back on, someone opened the door a crack. I couldn't see that ending well, but it was already too late. The face of a small girl peered through the opening and eyed our faces, then our hands. Then she saw the knocker Lorraine was holding and opened her eyes wide.

"Wait, no! Hold on a second. You see, this was, well, it was already broken!"

Lorraine made excuses, but the girl was calm. "Everyone says how we need to fix that thing. It startled you when it came off, didn't it? I'm sorry."

That was surprising to hear.

"It needed to be fixed? So it really was already broken?"

"It was. But a little adhesive is enough for it to stick on, so we left it like that."

That meant that whenever it came off, they did the same thing we were doing.

Lorraine slumped her shoulders. "You should've said so sooner," she grumbled.

"Once upon a time, there was a man."

The orphan girl guided us to a chapel inside the orphanage. When we got there, Alize opened a book and read a story loud and clear for the little children. It was a well-known tale.

"'The Westbound Traveler?' So they tell that story in Yaaran too, then," Lorraine whispered, mentioning the title of the story.

It was a famous fairy tale in Yaaran, known by children and adults alike. The premise was simple: a traveler heads west and meets a variety of people, solving their assorted problems. The reason why he was heading west was unknown. That problem was exacerbated by how each family had its own version of the story. Depending on who was telling the story, the reason for his journey differed. Sometimes the changes expressed the family's traditions and contained some interesting elements. Most of the time, the traveler was off to see his girlfriend or wife. Similar versions had him on a journey to meet with his siblings, parents, or other family members.

I was curious about what version Lorraine heard growing up. "Lorraine, why was the traveler heading west where you're from?"

"Me? For me, he wanted to meet the All-Knowing Sage. One day, the traveler realized he knew nothing, so he headed west. That's where a sage with the answers to all the world's questions lived, according to the story I heard."

It was a predictable answer coming from Lorraine. Maybe that story was why she grew up to be this way.

The look on my face must have told her what I was thinking. She asked me the same question. "Well, what about you? Why was the traveler heading west in your version?"

"Oh, it might've been a bit odd where I'm from."

"What's that mean?" Lorraine looked curious.

"Nothing. The traveler had no goal. If anything, he went west in search of one. He thought there could be something there."

Lorraine was at a loss for words. After a while, she nodded and said, "That might be interesting in itself. It's the answer I'd expect from an adventurer. I see, that's the kind of story a man like you could be raised on. Makes sense."

Her reply was reasonable. Stories alone wouldn't determine anyone's course in life, but I supposed they occupied some part of your mind. That was why you could see a hint of them in your personality.

"How do you think Alize is going to tell it?" I whispered. The traveler's objective is what I meant.

Lorraine considered the question. "Well, Alize is a girl. The traveler will probably be looking for a girlfriend. You know how it is."

And in order to do that, he would have to overcome trials over the course of a journey. The traveler was male in most tellings, but some bolder types also changed that element. Therefore, stories where the traveler wanted to see their significant other could play out either as a male traveler struggling for the sake of his girlfriend, or a female traveler doing the same for her boyfriend. They were both common archetypes popular with young girls. Boys, however, didn't take well to these versions. Love seemed to be foreign to them at that age. In that regard, girls were more mature. You could see the difference in how boys and girls grew up through these tales.

"Alize doesn't seem like she'd be obsessed with love, though," I reflected.

"You think so?"

"She takes things as they come, sort of. It's like she tries to act older than she is."

My evaluation convinced Lorraine. "Oh, I see what you mean. When you have to toil at a young age, it tends to make you a realist. You're saying Alize is that way?"

"Right, yeah." I didn't know how to put it in words, so Lorraine's eloquent description impressed me. I nodded in agreement.

But Lorraine was hesitant to concede. "That may be all the more reason for her to wait for a knight in shining armor, though," she said.

I couldn't say she was wrong. But there was only one way to tell.

"We'll find out from her story. Let's have a seat and listen for a bit."

We tiptoed into the chapel and sat near the wall. Lorraine and I both had ample experience as adventurers, so avoiding the attention of orphan children was simple enough to do in our sleep. Alize didn't notice us at all as she continued to read.

"The man's life continued as such until he had an idea: he could go on a journey to the west." She was still at the start of the story.

Alize paused for a breath.

"Why'd he want to do that?" a young boy chimed in. Maybe he had heard other versions, or maybe it was simple curiosity.

This question would determine the course of the tale.

Alize answered the boy's query. "He was a chef. So he went west in search of new ingredients and recipes. The lands in the west had a very advanced culture, you see."

He was more driven by gluttony than lust. It was somewhat disappointing, but my expectations seemed to be spot on. Her realism caused her to pick food over love.

"I guess I lose this one. Not that it was a competition," Lorraine remarked, but she looked irked. I, on the other hand, gave her a victorious smirk. Lorraine ground her teeth.

Ignorant to our presence, Alize went on.

The man's route was not without its difficulties. Many hardships befell him.

On his way to the west, something stood in the middle of the path. Struck with curiosity, the man drew near. What he found surprised him. It was a red-eyed monster.

The monster spoke. "If you wish to pass, you must leave behind that which you hold most dear."

The man was disturbed, but he took out a kitchen knife and handed it over.

"What is this?"

"I'm a chef. Cooking requires a kitchen knife. That being the case, nothing is more important to me than this."

The monster was confounded. "I have no reason to accept this. Take it back. You may pass."

The man nodded and hurried onward.

"A kitchen knife? Well, I get it. You can't cook without one."

I nodded, but Lorraine wasn't so sure. "If you tear up some vegetables with your hands and toss them in a stir fry, they'll turn out just fine. The traveler was smart about how he got through that." She pointed out his surprising amount of cunning.

I had to admit she was right. But now the monster's brain seemed a little lacking. It was a fairy tale, so maybe I was overthinking it.

Alize continued.

The man continued on his way until he reached the end of the road. The lands beyond appeared to be an endless wasteland. There were monsters in that treacherous region, so it was no place for humans to go. The man recalled that before his journey, the villager who had taught him about the road had said as much. But the man had a goal. He had to go west to find new ingredients and recipes. There was no other way.

Determined, the man set forth. He proceeded through the badlands so long he lost track of the time. Eventually, he came across something. What was it? Intrigued, the man approached and found something quite out of place. It was a woman clad in white.

The woman spoke to the man. "If you turn back now, you can still make it home. Head straight in that direction if you wish to go back where you came from. But if you keep going forward, you may lose your life."

He didn't know how the woman would know that. But the man had a goal. He had to go west to find new ingredients and recipes. No threat to his life could put an end to his journey.

The man responded to the woman. "I'll be heading west regardless. I'm set on it," he declared.

The woman was disappointed. "Why? Nothing should be more important than your life. What are you going west for?"

"The west will have new ingredients and recipes. I'm a chef. I want to make people happy. It's something I'm willing to risk my life for."

The woman thought for a moment, then waved her hand. A kitchen and ingredients materialized in the empty wasteland. She looked to the startled man with a vague smile. "If you truly mean that, then treat me to your cooking. Prove yourself if you wish to pass."

The man had no idea why the woman made this demand. But as a chef, he couldn't turn down a request for food. Besides, his journey had gone on so long he hadn't touched a kitchen in ages. The man was happy to start cooking.

Later, after a table appeared from nowhere in front of the woman, he set an abundance of dishes upon it. "Bon appétit."

The woman nodded at the man's salutation and started to eat. She only nibbled the food at first, but she devoured it faster and faster until every dish was licked clean.

Satisfied, the woman addressed the man. "So you are indeed a chef. If you make it to the west, I'm sure you'll learn to cook even more scrumptious dishes. Allow me to grant you my blessing."

When she waved her arm, the man sparkled. His body felt lighter. Now he thought he could make it west with ease.

The woman continued. "I shall attend you," she said and closed her eyes. The next thing the man knew, she had split into four women. The first had a smile that was dark. The second had a smile that was serene. The third was a young girl, and her smile befitted her age. The fourth had a smile that oozed allure.

The women spoke in unison. "This girl will go with you. We pray your journey is a success." With that, the three older women left the youngest of them and disappeared to parts unknown.

The girl bowed and said, "Nice to meet you."

The man did likewise. Then the odd pair's journey began.

"Have you ever wondered where the other three women went?" I asked Lorraine.

For every version of the traveler, this part of the story stayed the same. But the other women never showed up after this segment. I always found it strange.

Lorraine offered her opinion. "Fairy tales feature a lot of metaphors. The woman probably wanted to help the man out of good faith, right? This is supposed to express that or something. The other three women likely display other elements of human nature. One of them seems like she'd be full of bad faith, don't you think? Even those with the best intentions have darkness in their hearts. But 'The Westbound Traveler' has many interpretations. I'm not an expert, so pick up a book on the subject if you're interested." She considered the question to an extent, but threw in the towel in the end.

I thought her take on it was somewhat eccentric, but I could see what she meant.

Alize kept reading.

The traveler went on to meet with and speak to a number of people, solve riddles, and overcome trials until he reached the west. He obtained the ingredients and recipes he sought, used his talent to turn those recipes into something even greater, and became famous over time. Many chefs gathered around the man. Crowned as king for his accomplishments, the man acquired territory and founded his own country. Known as the King of Chefs, he lived happily ever after.

"The end," Alize said as she closed the book.

It sounded like she was done. But something seemed off.

"Is that it?" I asked.

Lorraine answered. "Yeah. 'The Westbound Traveler' always ends when he founds a country. Some parts can vary, but not the conclusion."

"I see." I nodded but remained confused. The story I heard as a child continued until the country fell to ruin.

If a chef was the traveler, for example, once he mastered cooking, the man called chefs from around the world to create a nation built on cooking. This drew the ire of other countries. Their jealousy at the cooking talent in the man's country inspired them to attack and take it for themselves.

The man did not wish to fight, but he had no choice. In the end, the man's country was devastated, and the other countries were fatigued as well. The man's dream of making everyone happy through cooking had ended in failure. Left in despair, he departed from the country and disappeared to an unknown land.

The man's power had built that country. Now that he was gone, the country became wearier and wearier as people fought for control, until they were engulfed in the waves of history. Over time, even the country's name was forgotten. That was how the story would end.

"Did my parents make all that up?" It was a tragic way to end the story, but a more realistic one, I supposed. Still, something bothered me.

"Say something?" Lorraine asked.

"No, nothing. Anyway, let's go talk to Alize."

We stood up and walked toward her.

"You're both here? Need something today?" Alize asked as she looked at us.

"Yes, something," I responded.

"What, is it complicated?"

"I wouldn't say that, but we'll be out of town on business for a while. I wanted to tell you the lectures will be on hold for the time being," I informed her.

Alize looked shocked. "How long is a while? A year? Two?" she asked.

We had no intention of being away that long, so Lorraine shook her head and responded. "No, no, about two weeks. We'll be back to teach plenty more before long."

Alize was relieved. "Thank goodness. I was so convinced you were going away forever. If that's all, then that's perfectly fine," she said.

Not that I wanted to leave town for such a long time, but I wondered why she thought I would. I couldn't help but ask. "Why would we go away forever?"

"Because you're trying to become a Mithril-class adventurer, aren't you? Then going to the capital would help you achieve that much faster. And Professor Lorraine is an incredible mage, not to mention an excellent scholar. I worry you'd be better off in the big city than out here in the middle of nowhere."

That was understandable. I had thought about moving at some point. But that was a long way off.

In any case, Alize's impression of me didn't seem to match her thoughts on Lorraine. I was only attempting to achieve something in her eyes, while Lorraine was already accomplished. Well, she wasn't wrong.

Lorraine laughed at Alize's concerns. "I'm not that great of a scholar. I do think my magic is decent enough, but it's not that special either. Same goes for Rentt. He wants to reach Mithril-class, yes, but is he good enough to get by in the capital? Not quite, as far as I'm concerned. We'll teach you the basics of being a mage and an adventurer before we leave for good," she declared.

That was the plan. The basics wouldn't take long to learn, so we had every intention of taking our time. A year might have been too long, but if we left for a few months and occasionally returned to teach her bit by bit, that would be fine. In that sense, Alize had no need to worry.

She nodded to Lorraine. "That's good. If you both went away, I don't think I could ever become an adventurer," she asserted.

"Really? Well, even if that doesn't work out, I imagine you could be a storyteller or a bard. Judging by that reading you just did, at least," Lorraine joked.

Only then did Alize realize we had been there for the story. She blushed. "You heard that? How embarrassing."

I consoled her. "It's nothing to be ashamed of. Making the traveler a chef is an interesting choice, though. Are you obsessed with food?"

"Rentt! I most certainly am not, but if there were a nation of cooking, I might like to visit," she said with a smile.

A nation of cooking? No such place existed, of course. It was all conceived from Alize's imagination. But a land where you could eat all the food in the world would be a dream come true. Even adults would want to go there. Aristocrats were always in search of delicacies, so they bought fresh monster parts for ludicrous prices. There wasn't much but Orc meat in the area, but other regions had a wider variety. That included moving mushrooms and flying fish.

"This discussion is making me hungry. Oh well. Alize, it doesn't have to be right now, but can I ask for a bit of your time?" I asked.

"For what?" Alize questioned me in return.

"I want to make some equipment for you. I already acquired the materials, but you need to go to the blacksmith to get your measurements taken. I also have plans to get a magic catalyst made. We could also do that today, if you want."

I didn't expect her to take the sudden invitation, though. All I wanted was to inform her there would be no lecture today, and to ask what day she would be available. It would be easiest if we could get it done right away, but that was a lot to ask. Alize was busy with her own matters.

But then she surprised me. "Hm. I don't have anything scheduled for today, so it'd probably be fine. The thing is, I'll have to ask Lady Lillian before I can give you my answer," she told me.

We didn't have all the time in the world, but a little waiting wouldn't be a problem. If it didn't work out, we could use the day to go shopping for assorted goods for the journey instead. So we nodded.

"All right, no problem. We'll wait here," I replied.

"Okay, got it. Then give me a second!" Alize said and left the chapel.

Alize returned some time later. She was free to go out that day, so we decided to visit the blacksmith together. When that finished, I was going to create a wand from parts of the Jyulapus Ents I defeated.

It wasn't just for Alize, though. Over the two-week journey to come, I wanted to practice magic using a catalyst, so I had cause to get a wand for myself.

"Oh, Rentt and Lorraine. Err..."

It had been some time since we visited Clope's Three-Pronged Harpoon. Upon entry, we were greeted by Luka, Clope's wife who was tending to the store.

When she saw my face, her expression filled with shock, confusion, and some nostalgia. My mask covered only half of my face now, so I expect that was why. I hadn't shown my old face around there in a while, hence her reaction.

"Hey, long time no see. This is Alize. She's our disciple. We're here for some equipment. Is Clope around?" I asked.

"Ah, yes, give me a moment. I'll go get him. Dear! Dear!!!" Luka ran to the forge in the back room and shouted.

Lorraine watched her go. "Are you sure you want them to see your face?" she asked tersely.

"Well, I'm sure it's fine. Hiding my face didn't sit well with me. I'm not worried about it anymore. It's not an issue."

I kept it vague because Alize was present, but Lorraine knew what I meant. I used to be a mere Undead, but by this point, I looked like an ordinary human. The Holy Fire had also cleared up suspicions about me being a vampire, so I figured I wouldn't bring any trouble anymore.

Alize cocked her head, but she was as understanding as ever. She got the sense our conversation was none of her business and moved away from us to observe the equipment around the store.

"I see. You should be able to straighten out your registration at the adventurer's guild somehow too, so it should be okay," Lorraine said and nodded, knowing how many holes there were in the guild's registration process.

I nodded back and approached Alize as she looked over the store's equipment. "See anything you like?" I asked.

Alize chose not to touch upon my conversation with Lorraine. "I'm not sure, but I don't think I could use anything too heavy."

She looked to a hulking greatsword. It would have been rough to handle, even for me. I was strong enough to hold it at this point, and could likely even swing it, but I didn't have the courage to use it as a solo adventurer. Alize would no doubt be crushed under its weight.

"Well, you don't have to worry about these enormous things. Besides, this blacksmith you're about to meet is a veteran. I'd ask him for advice before making any decisions."

"Really? Will you and Professor Lorraine help me too?" Alize inquired, sounding like the disciple she was.

I showed my approval. "Of course."

"You sure you should do that?" Clope asked as he walked in. I assumed he meant to ask why I was showing my face.

"When I'm outside, I generally cover my whole face like this," I responded and fiddled with the mask to reshape it to cover everything, painting my face to look like a skull.

"Never realized that mask was anything special. Hey, take it off and show it to me," Clope demanded.

After he mentioned it, I realized I most likely never told Clope about the mask. He was a talented blacksmith with an eye for more than weapons and armor, but I speculated this mask was too unusual for him. He might have been able to tell it was some sort of magic item, but he would never figure out its effects.

I had researched it myself and asked Lorraine for help to no avail, after all. I doubted anyone knew what it was.

"Take it off if you can. Then I'll be happy to show it to you," I smirked. He couldn't see my face, but my eyes showed I was smiling.

Up to the challenge, Clope rolled up his sleeves. "What? All right, if you insist," he said and approached me to put his hands on each side of the mask.

Clope yanked with all his might, but it didn't budge. All he managed to do was pull on my skin and hurt my face. As with most blacksmiths, Clope had strong arms. Creating equipment that could survive throughout adventures demanded a fair amount of power. Clope was skinny at a glance, yet muscular and tough. And this was the man tugging on an object stuck to my face, so you can imagine the agony. But I was a vampire of sorts, so my endurance and restorative abilities were high. My skin would have been torn off otherwise. For a moment I was glad I had become a monster, but after I thought about it rationally, that was also the only reason I wore this mask.

"I think that's enough," I told Clope after I got fed up.

"Huh? Oh," he sighed and took his hands off me. "But dang, it's really stuck on there. What the hell's with that mask?"

"I don't know. I believe it was bought from a street vendor, but I haven't been able to take it off since I put it on. At least it gives me an excuse not to remove it, and I can change its appearance, so it's not so bad. But ideally I don't want to have to wear this for the rest of my life."

Adventurers often wore masks, but I had no need for one. Besides, while I didn't mind wearing it on adventures, the inability to take it off while sleeping or bathing was irksome. I was starting to get used to it, but if it could be removed, I would jump on the opportunity.

"Sounds to me like it's cursed. If it's not too strong of a curse, a little divinity cleansing should do the trick, but you could've done that yourself," Clope surmised, knowing I could use divinity.

"I tried it. Didn't work. Someone else even happened to do it for me, but nothing happened." Saint Myullias had blessed my entire body with divinity, which did have a cleansing effect. But in the end, the mask stayed on. There was also Nive's Holy Fire, but that was distinct from cleansing. In any case, it wasn't coming off, and there was no use thinking about it.

"So typical cleansing doesn't work, eh?"

"Right."

"Huh. Lorraine, you know a way to get it off?" Clope directed his attention to her.

She shook her head. "If I did, I would've done it by now. I looked into it but didn't find much."

Lorraine was also an adventurer, and while she almost always carried out requests in her robes, she did wear light armor underneath. She carried a dagger for close combat and dissection as well, so she came to this blacksmith on occasion and was acquainted with Clope.

He looked conflicted by her answer. "Yeah? You couldn't do it either? I'll try and check it out a bit more," he concluded and then looked behind us to where Alize was hiding. "So, just something for her today?"

Alize had concealed herself because of Clope's somewhat aggressive appearance. He was thin but intense. Once he laid his eyes on something, he never looked away. Young girls must have found him frightening.

"Alize, it's okay. He's nicer than he looks. Besides, if Rentt didn't scare you, why this ordinary man? Isn't that silly?" Lorraine pointed out as she pushed Alize forward. If you had to pick what was scarier between a man in dark robes and a skull mask and a loud-mouthed tough guy, it might be harder than you think. We inspired different types of fear. Not that it mattered.

"Alize, this is Clope, a blacksmith who's been helping me out since before I became an adventurer. Like Lorraine said, he's not as scary as he looks. He'll be making your equipment," I told Alize.

She resolved herself and stepped toward him. "I'm Alize, a kid from the Second Orphanage of Maalt and a disciple of Rentt and Professor Lorraine. Nice to meet you," she offered. She had been formal with me too when I had first come to the orphanage, so that was nothing unexpected from her. But unlike then, she was with people she could depend on, so her behavior was a bit more shy. That must have meant when I had gone to the orphanage, she had been pushing herself past her boundaries. When I thought about how much I must have scared her, I felt bad. It was too late for that now, however.

"Hoh, a kid that's not scared of me. Don't see that often. All right, nice to meet you too. So I just need to make equipment for you, then?" Clope said and patted Alize on the head. He was always warmhearted toward women and children. That was how he had a beautiful wife like Luka. And if you looked closer at his stern face, it was rather handsome and refined.

People used to say I had a baby face. I wondered what they'd say now. I was paler, and I felt my eyes looked sharper, so I suspected I no longer seemed so young. As for Lorraine, she was a grown woman from any angle. Whether she looked her age was hard to say, though. You could say she was an intellectual beauty of indeterminate age. It seemed like the passage of time would have no effect on her looks. It was enough to make me jealous. Not that I would age anymore either, as far as I knew.

"Yes!" Alize shouted back at Clope.

"Yeah, and as for the materials, I picked some up in a dungeon. Could you start by looking at those?" I chimed in.

Clope raised an eyebrow. "Yeah? You can actually go to those dungeons now? Color me impressed. All right, then come with me, everyone. I'll take you to the forge," Clope said and walked off. We followed behind him.

I had been to this forge many times. It featured little I hadn't seen before, but Alize saw it differently. Her eyes sparkled as she looked around. You wouldn't have much reason to enter a forge if you weren't an adventurer or a knight, so her reaction was to be expected.

Her gender could've also been a reason for her reaction. Clope let Lorraine into the forge too, so he didn't have any holdups about that, but some blacksmiths refused to allow women into their forges. There were a plethora of reasons, but they often said that while the Blacksmithing Deity didn't care, the Furnace Deity was a woman who got jealous of other women. Whether the Furnace Deity was male or female was up for debate, but it wasn't worth arguing with people over their faith. These ideas were held by many, so women seldom had the opportunity to see a forge. When I considered that, Alize's feelings were easy to understand.

"Leave the goods there," Clope said and pointed to a large table. It appeared to be a stand used for processing materials, and it looked sturdy enough to hold ingots without an issue. I took the items out of my magic pouch and set them down.

"Mana iron? That means you went to the New Moon Dungeon? Or Hamdan Mine?" Clope asked while looking at the metal. Any blacksmith in this town would have to know where materials were available in the surrounding area. His knowledge of ore was comprehensive, no doubt.

He was right to guess the New Moon Dungeon, but Hamdan Mine was a small mine about two days away from Maalt. It had been abandoned long ago, so only adventurers went there anymore. There was supposed to be mana iron in there still, but monsters dwelled there as well, and the tunnels had grown old and decrepit. Most of the mine's value had been extracted, at which point it was abandoned, as far as I had heard. Even so, the only places around Maalt where mana iron could be found were the New Moon Dungeon and Hamdan Mine.

"I went to the New Moon Dungeon. I picked it up on the fourth floor," I responded.

"The fourth floor? You were only ever able to get to maybe the second by yourself. Well, this is what makes smithing so much fun," Clope said with a smile. He seemed happy about my progress. It wasn't so much thanks to personal growth as it was a factor of me becoming a monster, but I didn't need to mention that. It would only complicate matters.

After I took out all the regular mana iron, I took out the metal tinged with dragon mana. Clope opened his eyes wide.

"Is that brass? Wait, actually, Rentt, is this what I think it is?"

"This is mana iron too. I don't know why, but there was an earth dragon on the fourth floor. It had apparently been there so long it morphed the mana iron around it. I asked Lorraine about it, and presumably this is rare."

"Yeah, very rare. Dragons with enough mana to morph mana iron don't show up too often. But you sure you want to use this as material? If you put it up for auction, it'll fetch a high price."

It was only after Clope mentioned it that I considered that option. I figured I might as well ask how much money I could expect. "I have no intention of selling this, but for future reference, how much does it go for?"

"Hm? Well, if a blacksmith who knows his craft happens to be there, he'll probably pay a platinum coin for this one ingot."

A platinum coin was equal to a hundred gold coins. It was hard to say if that was expensive or cheap for this material, but it wasn't exactly a fortune. Normal mana iron sold for about a hundredth of the price, though.

"Meaning this metal has attributes worthy of that cost?" Lorraine asked.

Clope pondered the question. "It's tough to know for sure. Depends on how you use it, they say. Just hammering it into a weapon will get you somewhat better results than the standard mana iron, but that's about it. But there's supposedly a way to turn it into something special."

"That's awfully vague. How would you do that, precisely?" Lorraine questioned Clope further.

"Using this mana iron by itself isn't gonna produce much of anything. You need some other materials. For example, one process I know demands a magic crystal you won't get from anything weaker than Platinum-class monsters, and leaves from the Holy Tree. And if you're talking materials that are nearly impossible to get, it requires vampire blood too. That'd clearly be pretty rough, so I can't recommend you make equipment out of this."

It did sound like it would be difficult, but Clope didn't know how easily I could get vampire blood. I only had to use my own. Whether I was a vampire had become somewhat unclear, so maybe it wouldn't work, but it was worth a shot.

That only left the magic crystal and the Holy Tree leaves. Even in the worst-case scenario, I could save up enough money for the crystal. As for sacred trees, I needed more information.

"By Holy Tree, do you mean the one in the Land of the Venerable Holy Tree?" I asked Clope.

"Yeah, the nation of the high elves. Good luck getting those."

"That does sound brutal."

The Land of the Venerable Holy Tree was ruled by high elves, and the majority of its population was elves as well. It was considered a nation, but most of its land was surrounded by forest, and they didn't have a government in the way human countries did. In reality, it was a group of settlements with tight connections that called themselves a country. But their borders were unclear to the point that it was hard to call them a country in the conventional sense. Because they were a venerable race who protected the Holy Tree, the name of their nation had been placed upon them by the ruler of some other nation long ago. The elves at the time didn't seem to mind the name.

Of course, I had never been to the country because I couldn't go if I wanted to. I didn't know how the elves drew their borders, and if a human set foot in a forest they claimed as their territory, they would be attacked. All elves were experts in spirit magic and experienced with bows and arrows, so a human who entered with no plan would be driven off. There wouldn't even be a fight. The Holy Tree was said to stand deep within the country, where it generated divinity at all times, so I had to wonder how many humans had ever seen it.

This talk of a tree that gave off divinity reminded me of something. "Clope, what happened to the tree that grew from the doll I cut?"

"Oh, that? It's growing nicely. You're not thinking of using that as a substitute for the Holy Tree, are you?"

I did consider it just a bit. I looked at Clope to see if he thought it was possible, but he shook his head.

"No way will that work. I don't know if it's because it was made from your divinity or what, but it does seem to give off some mild divinity. I figured that out when I held a cursed item close to the tree and it got cleansed, but that's the extent of what it can do. The real Holy Tree is supposed to vaporize any Undead that draws near it. A long while back, I saw Holy Tree leaves go up for auction, and I could feel the cleansing in the air from all the way in my seat. Your tree doesn't have that much power."

"So, what's the tree?" Lorraine asked. At first I thought she was asking a philosophical question about what trees were, but when I thought about it more, I realized that although I had told Lorraine about the effects of using spirit, mana, and divinity with my sword, I hadn't mentioned the tree that had grown from it.

Clope answered her before me. "Oh, Rentt here charged his sword with divinity and sliced a wooden doll, then a plant sprouted from it. I thought that was neat, so I'm taking care of the thing," he said plainly.

"Odd, but actually, it makes sense. Things grow wherever Rentt goes, after all. I agree, it is neat. Clope, could you show it to me?"

Lorraine smiled after making an old joke about me. She wasn't surprised to hear this because I had previously made plants grow with my wings. If my divinity could do that, then it could make plants sprout from wooden dolls.

"Fine with me. Hold on a sec," Clope told Lorraine.

Some time later, he came in with a flower pot containing the tree. It had grown to around half my height. Not much time had passed since it first sprouted, so that seemed fast to me.

"Here it is. So, feel anything from it?" Clope asked us.

Lorraine was the first to speak. "I don't sense any divinity. I feel like it cleaned up the air a bit, but that's all."

"I think the same thing," Alize commented after Lorraine.

I answered last. "It does seem to give off a small amount of divinity. The same as me," I said. My divinity gave me the ability to see other divinity to an extent, so a misty glow was visible around the tree. Even so, it was no great amount.

"So it really is the same? Then maybe the divinity's making it grow fast because it's a plant. This flower pot is gonna be a bit tight before long, but I don't know about planting it in the ground."

Clope's store was by no means small, but all the space was used up for his smithing business. The courtyard was also used to test weapons, leaving nowhere to plant the tree. A normal tree might be able to grow around the edges of the courtyard, but this one was special. It appeared to grow at a considerable speed, so planting it without a plan could end poorly. This tree was born from my divinity, yet it was almost cursed. I felt bad about it, to be honest. But Clope was the one who wanted to care for it, so I had no sympathy for him. He should have thrown it out right away.

"That said, it still seems to be doing all right. If it does get to the point where you can't care for it anymore, why not go plant it on some mountain?" I suggested.

"Might have to do that in the end, but I could get some use out of it. Maybe it won't work as a replacement for the Holy Tree, but I'll bet I can make some equipment out of the wood. It'll take some experimenting to know what effects it'll have, though."

"That's a fascinating idea. It could be used for alchemy as well. Clope, will you share some with me?" Lorraine requested, her curiosity piqued.

Materials with divinity were hard to come by. Many were highly sought after, such as the leaves and branches of the Holy Tree. More common examples included holy water sold by a church or items a saint filled with their power. The latter were easier to procure, so I thought they were better off using those. But when I asked them about it, Clope looked unsure.

"Holy water is made with the Church's secret techniques. Using the divinity from that for anything but its intended purpose isn't easy."

Lorraine made a face much like Clope's. "The items that saints make are the same way. They're careful about leaks revolving around that."

If it were possible to utilize that divinity for anything, then selling those items might not have been so great for their religious organization. That divinity could only be produced by saints in the first place, so I didn't think it made much of a difference, but presumably it wasn't so simple. For example, someone like Lorraine could discover the mechanisms of that divinity and learn to mass-produce items that performed cleansing and healing without the need for a saint. It wouldn't be as easy as that, but it wouldn't be impossible either. Healing and cleansing items turned up in dungeons on occasion, after all. Less effective imitations of those items were also made and sold by your average magic item shops. The more effective versions required rare materials to create, so they were no replacement for saints, but they could be one day. That must have been why they kept the creation of these items a secret.

"Still, it's not totally impossible, but Rentt's tree here should certainly be easier to use. So, how about it?" Lorraine asked.

I got the feeling they wanted to use the tree I made as a divinity generator. That sounded about right.

Clope nodded at Lorraine. "That's all good with me. This isn't the only tree, actually. There's another four of them. You can have two."

I was surprised to hear that he had that many, but at the time there were even more sprouts from the doll than that. Maybe he had tried to plant them all, and that was how so many survived. But out of five total, he was only giving up two? Not that I had any complaints, but it sounded like he was having trouble caring for them, so I would have thought he'd hand over all but one.

With a number of concerns, I asked, "You'll be okay with three of them?"

"Shouldn't be an issue. I could chop them up for firewood if it comes down to it. Might be disrespectful to use trees full of divinity for that, but that divinity came from you anyway. Not exactly blasphemous or anything," he said.

If you went back further, my divinity came from a divine spirit, so it was somewhat blasphemous. But I wasn't that devout, so it was hard to care. Whether someone chose to believe in a god was up to them. To begin with, the degree to which the gods themselves were concerned with the affairs of mankind had been a subject of debate for ages. An extreme argument would suggest they hadn't the least interest in the actions of humans, including murder, opting instead to sit back and watch our lives unfold. By that logic, the burning of a tree wouldn't faze them, so I didn't see any problem.

In fact, if burning trees meant anything to the gods, humanity would have perished a long time ago. Everybody used firewood.

"Talk to me before you burn them. I'm willing to go plant them in the forest at any time." I didn't think it was that necessary, but these trees had grown from my divinity. They felt like my children, on some level.

"Then I'll do that if the time comes for it. Anyway, we're way off topic, so let's get back to the young lady's equipment. First of all, what kind of equipment do you want?" Clope asked and brought out a few basic weapons.

"Give these a try," Clope said and tossed the weapons on the table. There was a wide variety, some of which would be absurd to recommend to a beginner. The chakram in particular.

"Um, I don't know where to start," Alize murmured.

It made sense that someone who had never bought a weapon before would be at a loss. Back when I was starting out, I had learned how to fight from a hunter. My primary weapons had been a bow and a knife, much like a hunter, so I never had to think about it. By the time I decided to become an adventurer, I was experienced with a knife and had taught myself to use a sword. I got most of the fundamentals down back then. In other words, I never had to make a choice, for better or worse.

Later on, I asked an adventurer who sometimes came to town as a traveling merchant's bodyguard to teach me common sword techniques so I could learn more. When I became decent enough at fighting, the person teaching me got more into it as well, as I recall. One day, however, he stopped coming to town, replaced by someone else. Whether he died on a mission or left for another land, I didn't know. He wasn't an adventurer from Maalt, so it was hopeless to try and investigate it in town. If I checked a regional guild headquarters in a bigger city, maybe I could determine his whereabouts, but that might take some time. Besides, at the time, the adventurer had said, "I'll see you if I see you, I won't if I don't." He was a strangely aimless man, but now I understood how he felt. That was the main reason I didn't think more about looking for him.

In any case, Alize wasn't so limited by her background, but the freedom of choice made matters more difficult. It was times like these when you needed a mentor's advice.

Lorraine threw out some random guidance. "Hm, you can use magic, so I imagine that will be your main form of ranged attack. If your weapon will mainly be used for close combat, maybe you should pick with that in mind."

"Oh, you have mana? Then you won't be needing these," Clope said and removed the bows, chakrams, and other ranged weaponry. That left only the typical close combat weapons: swords, daggers, spears, axes, greatswords, and so forth.

"I'm not sure I can hold that," Alize said as she reached out to the greatsword and tried to pick it up. It wasn't as hard as she thought. A child of twelve could hold a greatsword with some effort, but she wobbled to a dangerous degree.

"This is a no-go too, then," Clope said as he plucked the greatsword from the stumbling girl's hands and set it aside. A blacksmith with no strength would have no place in the business, so his muscles were nothing to scoff at. He could handle a greatsword with no problem.

"You use one of these, don't you, Rentt?" Alize asked and picked up a sword.

I didn't have to mention it was my main weapon, but I did have something else to say about that. "It's not like that's all I use. I can wield all kinds of weapons," I said and picked up spears and axes, showing her the proper stances for each of them to show off.

"Wow! You can do anything, Rentt," Alize complimented me. It got to my head until Clope had to say something.

"Waste of talent, that's what he is," Clope said exasperatedly.

"If anyone's a jack of all trades and master of none, Rentt is. Every household could use one of him," Lorraine joked.

"I can fight pretty well now, I'll have you know," I objected, a bit annoyed.

"Obviously I'm aware of that. I'm kidding. That's all Rentt can do, though, so you don't need to choose a weapon just because Rentt did," Lorraine said to Alize. Lorraine had inferred that she might choose a sword because it was my main weapon and offered her own advice.

This wasn't something most children would have to mull over, but knowing Alize's background, it was only natural. Alize was an orphan, one who had to satisfy others in order to survive, so when given a choice like this, she found it hard to make a decision. We knew that and joked around to help the mood. Lorraine was quick to understand, and Clope's love of children made him surprisingly good at it.

Her eyes opened a little wider. "Really?" Alize asked.

"Yeah, of course. It can be a spear or bow or axe or anything. Whatever it is, I can teach you. I might not be top-class at any of that, though." I was going to say I could make her a top-class adventurer instead, but I couldn't bring myself to say it.

Clope spoke up instead. "Well, no reason to make fun of him. This guy loves practicing his stances and fundamentals all day long.

Seeing how he moves now, I doubt there'd be anyone better to teach you the basics. He's smooth and resolute," Clope said with praise.

I didn't think I was so great, though. I was still only a Bronze-class, but it did make me happy to hear that.

"That's more praise than I deserve. I'm decent, but don't expect too much. I think I can turn you into a competent adventurer, but whether you become a first-rate one will depend on your effort and talent. Don't forget that," I lectured to Alize.

"Okay. Don't worry, I know," she promptly answered.

In the end, it seemed Alize saw me as a third-rate adventurer. I was disappointed for a moment by that, but I didn't have much time to dwell on it before she continued.

"I like embroidering, and that involves weaving together thin strings into a big pattern. If you're careful about it, you can create wonderful art, but it takes a lot of time and effort. Adventurers are the same way, aren't they? You've been working at this for long enough to get strong, but I haven't done much of anything yet," she said humbly.

I didn't know if I deserved such a nice, thoughtful girl as a disciple. Maybe I should have gone straight to the capital, knocked on the doors of every top-class adventurer, and begged them to take her as their disciple instead. That idea did occur to me for a second, but I couldn't do that. I had decided to teach Alize, so it was my responsibility to train her. At the very least, I had to keep at it until she had the knowledge and skills to stand on her own as an adventurer. That wasn't why I said what I said next, but I found myself blurting it out.

"Just the other day, you learned all the basics of magic from Lorraine, didn't you? You're doing the best you can. If you keep this up, you'll surpass me in no time." It was almost something an obsessive parent might say. Maybe something was wrong with me.

Alize looked at two weapons, lost in thought. She had tested enough to know which wouldn't work, thereby cutting the selection down through the process of elimination.

"A dagger and a sword? You can't pick which one?" I asked.

"Yeah. The dagger is easier to carry, which sounds like a good fit for me, but the sword might be easier to use once I'm an adventurer." In other words, she personally preferred the dagger but felt the sword would be more useful in reality.

Her conundrum was easy to understand, and she was right to think how she did. Monsters were dangerous. Goblins could be dispatched easily enough, but orcs had thick fat and muscle, while slimes were gelatinous and amorphous. Daggers would have trouble against them. You needed something with a longer blade.

However, Alize knew magic. Little more than life magic at the moment, but once she learned even the lowest level offensive spells, she would be more than capable of fighting orcs and slimes. If anything, slimes were best dealt with by using magic. For Alize, a weapon would be a last resort for when an enemy got too close.

That was the approach of many adventurers, but I did want her to fight with a weapon too. Maybe that was my mentorly ego talking. Knowing this, I didn't offer a recommendation either way. I wanted her to pick for herself, but there was one piece of advice I could think of. When I looked at Lorraine's face, it looked like she had the same idea. We nodded to each other.

"Alize, I think it's fine if you pick either, but I want to show you something that could help you decide. Lorraine."

When I said her name, Lorraine picked up the dagger. "Watch this," she said, then she charged the blade with mana. Rather, she activated a spell. The tip of the dagger sprouted a transparent blade. Lorraine structured the spell to make it clear this blade had some sort of physical form despite being see-through, so it reflected the light in the room. It was about the length of the sword.

"Lorraine," Clope said before he set a small log on the table.

"Alize, stand back a bit. Here goes nothing," Lorraine warned and then struck the log with a horizontal slash. The dagger itself didn't touch the log at all, only the transparent part. A fissure appeared in the log at a slight slant, leaving it split in two.

The way she slashed was awe-inspiring, as it should have been, since I was the one who had taught her how. She was faster than I had been when I was human, I was sad to admit, but Lorraine excelled at magic, so enhancing her physical abilities was well within her grasp. She could have made it even stronger, but there was no need for that now.

"What was that?" Alize asked.

"Magic," Lorraine answered. "I extended the blade of the dagger to the length of a sword. This isn't an especially difficult spell, so you should be able to make do with a dagger."

Overall, it was best to pick what you liked. You would learn faster that way. If she wanted to pick the dagger but thought the blade of a sword would be better, then seeing how one weapon could fulfill both criteria might help her come to a decision. But while Lorraine said this wasn't difficult magic, I couldn't cast it. That was more an issue of my lack of mana, so maybe I could learn it now, but most of the adventurers who could cast it were at least Silver-class. That didn't make it sound simple to me.

"Lorraine, not to question you, but is this a spell Alize can learn?" I whispered.

"If she couldn't, I wouldn't have shown her this. She displayed plenty of potential with life magic the other day. If she can manage that, then she can learn this with enough studying," she whispered back.

That settled that. I turned back toward Alize. "So what did you think? Was that helpful?" I asked.

"Yeah. If I can do that, then I think the dagger is fine. Do you think so too?" She sounded set on it.

I nodded. "That sounds good. I'll just mention that if you want to learn that, you'll have to study with both swords and daggers, giving you twice the work. Is that okay with you?" I hated to say anything that might change her mind, but I had to bring it up. If she handled her weapon poorly and died because of it, this would all be meaningless. No small number of adventurers met that fate, but I had an inkling as to how Alize would respond.

"I don't know how it'll work out, but I'll do my best. I'm going to study the best I can to become an adventurer, so teach me well, Rentt."

"Of course. Lorraine and I will turn you into a full-fledged adventurer," I declared.

"And a mage and scholar, as well," Lorraine added.

"So, just want me to make a dagger, then?" Clope asked, but I shook my head.

"No, best to make a dagger and a sword. There are enough materials, right?" I said.

Clope was quick to pick up on my intentions. "Right, she'll have to learn to handle a sword too. And until she learns that spell, she needs to practice with the real thing."

"That's the idea. And knowing her way around a sword will broaden her skill set." A sword was the standard weapon of most adventurers. Knowing how to use one wouldn't hurt.

"Then I'll make both. Which mana iron should I use?" He meant between the normal mana iron and the one with dragon mana.

This was an obvious decision. "The normal mana iron, please."

"You sure? I thought you'd want to give her something nice."

"If Alize starts off using something too atypical, she'll develop strange habits. I'm keeping that in mind."

"Oh, I get that. All right then. But what do you want to do with this mana iron?" Clope asked and looked at the iron soaked with dragon mana.

"How much could you make from that? One dagger, or what?"

"Well, a little more than that, I think. Not as much as what normal mana iron could produce, but a fair amount. Enough that I'd have room for testing."

"In that case, can you try using one of those trees I made to create a sword out of it?"

"Hey, I told you it'd require more materials than that. Even ignoring the Holy Tree leaves, there's no way you're getting vampire blood. The crystal, too."

Vampire blood was something I could get. The magic crystal, on the other hand, might not be so easy.

"I'll do something about the vampire blood. As for the crystal—"

"'Do something?' Really, now?" Clope wanted to ask something, but I left him aside and kept talking.

"Would a magic crystal from a Tarasque work?" That was something I'd be able to collect. Not without some effort, but it was possible. They weren't quite Platinum-class, but they could be somewhere around Gold-class.

Clope thought for a moment before he answered. "It might work, but it'd be a waste of this mana iron. If you got the Holy Tree leaves and a Platinum-class magic crystal, I could make one hell of a sword."

"But do you expect me to ever get those materials?" Maybe I could one day, but not now. Clope seemed to know that too.

"Well, you got a point there. All right, I'll give it a shot. There should be some left over afterward anyway. I'll make sure there's still some remaining for when you come to me with the Holy Tree leaves one day," he said with a laugh.

Chapter 2: Making a Catalyst

In the end, we went with a sword and dagger for Alize. We told Clope and Luka we would be away from Maalt for a while, leaving them time to finish the weapons. Alize wouldn't get to use them until after Lorraine and I returned from Hathara anyway. That being said, we did have time for a bit of training before we left, but Alize could borrow a sword and dagger from one of us for that. We probably had some old, used equipment that would work for training but not so much for fighting monsters. That was good enough for the time being.

I consulted Clope about armor as well, but he told me Alize would be better off with leather armor or robes. Since daggers and magic would be her primary means of combat going forward, something lighter would be better. Clope referred us to another armor shop, but since there wasn't much time left in the day, we decided to visit another time. There was other business to attend to.

"Now it's time to make a magic catalyst. Ready, you two?" Lorraine asked.

We had left Clope's and returned to Lorraine's living room. Lorraine set up a big table and a writing board, and she held a stick as she walked us through it. The board was a magic item upon which words and images could be repeatedly drawn and erased. Lorraine felt the process of creating a wand would be most easily understood through visuals, so she had dragged the board out from somewhere.

I couldn't imagine it was cheap, but I wondered if all scholars owned one. Not that I would know, but Lorraine had one, so I assumed so.

"Yes, I'm ready!" Alize shouted.

Lorraine looked at her with satisfaction and then turned to me. "And what about you, Rentt?" she inquired.

"I'm ready, yes," I groaned.

"Put some life into it," she demanded, but I gave her a look of protest. She pointed to me with her stick. "Are you determined to refuse?"

I gave up resisting. "Yes, I'm ready!" I screamed as loud as my lungs would permit. Alize laughed.

We were, of course, joking around. Lorraine and I then returned to our usual demeanors, and the lecture continued.

"Well, it's nothing terribly difficult. Today I'll show you how to produce a wand, the most basic magic catalyst. Rings and weapons can also function as catalysts, to name just a couple others, but those are somewhat advanced. Either way, you should learn the basics before you try something more complex. Are you following so far?"

Lorraine watched us silently nod. "Good. Then let's begin right away. First, let me give you a demonstration." She reached into the bag of materials I had collected and took out some wood from a shrub ent and the magic crystal from an orc soldier.

"These are all the materials you need for a basic catalyst. Even this can have some depth if you want to go after the smaller details, but you don't need to know about that for now. All right, here goes. First, I'll draw a magic circle on this board," Lorraine said and hit the writing board with her stick. A simple magic circle made up of circles, triangles, and squares appeared. Next, she used an ink brush to draw the same circle on a board on the table. The board appeared to be made of bronze, and the ink circle settled into the surface.

"Give it a touch," Lorraine said, so Alize did. The ink had already dried like the pattern was part of the board, much to her surprise.

"Is there something special about this board?" Alize asked, but Lorraine shook her head.

"No, it's an ordinary bronze board. The ink is what's special. It's made just for drawing magic circles. Not that you couldn't go without it, but it soaks into the material in such a way that you don't have to worry about it smudging or disappearing later. It raises the chance of success, essentially."

The ink was available at most magic item shops, but only mages and alchemists tended to buy it due to its high price. Besides, writing and erasing with it required magic, so it was hard for the average citizen to use. I assumed that was why Alize didn't know about it.

"I see," Alize said with a nod.

"Next, I'll pour mana into the magic circle. Here goes," Lorraine said, touching the board.

The way she offered her mana looked effortless, but it wasn't. Lorraine had just done it enough times to make it seem simple. Alize and I would need practice before we could do this, that was clear at a glance, but Alize didn't seem to know that yet.

"It looks so simple," she said.

It wasn't. This alone would take a while to learn, but Lorraine was somewhat mischievous when it came to these matters.

"Yeah, simple," she told Alize. I didn't know if she was serious or if she intended to make Alize toil to learn this in a short time. Either way, it was a frightening statement.

"So, next," Lorraine said when the magic circle had received enough mana. She picked up the magic crystal and set it on the circle. It began to glow.

"Wow," Alize whispered.

"You can't use raw magic crystals as catalysts, so we have them absorb these magic circles. We could simply leave it sitting for a while, but let's get it over with quickly today," Lorraine said and held her hands right in front of the magic crystal. She then manipulated the mana again. The magic crystal shone brighter for a few seconds before the light disappeared, at which time Lorraine picked it up and looked at it.

"Yes, this will do. Would you like to have a look?" she asked and handed the magic crystal to Alize, who looked at it with mild shock.

"What is it?" I asked.

"The magic circle is in the magic crystal," she proclaimed and then handed it to me.

Just like Alize said, the magic circle was now rotating inside the magic crystal. This was what Lorraine had meant by it being absorbed. I was used to this sight, though, so it didn't surprise me. I still couldn't create any magic items, but I had gotten good enough at judging them. The pragmatic side of my adventurer spirit had to ask how much this might sell for. The wand this magic crystal was being used for probably wouldn't be worth much.

That reminded me of something. "Alize, have Lorraine show you one of her wands. It's neat," I suggested. Lorraine had a heap of staves, rings, and other magic catalysts. I thought it might be nice to let Alize see one she regularly used.

"Right, that might make things easier to understand. Here," Lorraine said and then grabbed a wand leaning against the wall and handed it to Alize.

"Alize, look at the magic crystal on it," I recommended.

"Wow, this is amazing!" she exclaimed and opened her eyes even wider than a moment ago.

"Right?" I said.

Alize nodded and peered at the magic crystal again. "There's so many magic circles, and they're folded together so they look kind of spherical," she observed as she gave me the wand.

I knew what was there, but I took a look while I had the opportunity. Magic circles far more intricate than the one Lorraine had just created were packed inside. And they were all interconnected to form orbs, totaling three in all. Each orb remained far enough from the others to not touch them, and they all rotated in different directions. It was like looking at an hourglass, hypnotic enough that I could keep watching it forever.

"These are called three-dimensional layered magic circles. By structuring the magic circles three-dimensionally, it's possible to write in more information. Magic circles contain information in each individual pattern and character, and it's a challenge to see how efficiently they can be assembled. Three-dimensional shapes can store far more information, of course. If you want to get more complicated, there are multi-dimensional layered magic circles, which are four-dimensional— Oh."

Lorraine paused when she noticed Alize was getting increasingly confused. I knew how she felt. I learned a lot from the books I'd borrowed from Lorraine, but Alize had grown up in an orphanage, so this had to be rough for her to follow. Lorraine seemed to get the same idea.

"Sorry. This would be easier to understand if I taught you math first. I was talking to you like I talk to Rentt. That's not right," Lorraine apologized.

Alize shook her head. "No, I at least got the sense that it's something remarkable. Rentt, do you understand this complicated language?" Alize asked.

"More or less. Reading Lorraine's books happens to be a hobby of mine. I've been doing that for a decade, so I've learned a thing or two," I said.

As to how much I'd learned specifically, a commoner would see me as fairly informed. For someone like Lorraine, however, I couldn't do much more than talk to them. I did have a great deal of adventurer-related knowledge pertaining to this city, but academics were outside my field of expertise. Back in my hometown of Hathara, the mayor and an old medicine woman had taught me some fundamental academics, which was enough to read Lorraine's books by myself, but that was nothing special.

Lorraine disagreed. "Rentt's pretty good. How a man like him was raised in a village in the middle of nowhere is a mystery," she said, complimenting me.

It was a mystery to her because I hardly talked about my origins or my hometown. I had mentioned the medicine woman and the mayor's teachings in passing, but that was it. Lorraine never tried to pry either. Adventurers tended to have a history they'd rather keep secret. If one chose not to discuss their past, then others shouldn't ask.

"Well, enough about me. Let's get back to making that wand," I said.

Lorraine took a step back. "Right. I stopped at putting a magic circle in the magic crystal, I believe. The next step is dealing with the grip of the wand, but there are many ways to go about this."

"Really?" Alize asked.

"Yes. For example, the most old-fashioned way is to shave it down by hand. You can use a knife or other tool to shape it as you see fit. That's how it was done in the past, but it takes ages, and mistakes can have disastrous results. I wouldn't recommend it, but a skilled craftsman can create wands of the highest caliber that way. You could try it if you plan to become an artisan, but we're focusing on the basics right now, so you don't need to go that route," Lorraine rambled.

"The easier and more widely known method is to shape your wand with magic. For example, you can do this," she said as she began to pour mana into the shrub ent wood. She watched until it was filled with enough mana, and then she employed the mana to peel off a part of the wood and make it float in the air. It was the length of an average wand, around 30 centimeters. She manipulated the mana further to reshape that part bit by bit. Mana wrapped around the wood like a spiral, gradually shaping it into a wand. It was structured so the bark formed the outside surface of the wand, and the shape went from thin on one end to increasingly thicker as it approached the other. This could be called the work of a craftsman.

"Here comes the hardest part. The magic crystal and the wand have to be combined. Here goes nothing." Lorraine poured mana into the magic crystal with one hand and into the wand with the other, making them float and approach each other. Light blue sparks flew from the tip of the wand, and when the magic crystal drew near, it latched onto the wood. Once fully joined, the wood around the tip of the wand shifted and wrapped around the crystal.

As Lorraine picked up the wand, the light from it and the magic crystal faded away. "Well, that's how it's done. It came out okay, I suppose," she muttered and looked at the wand from multiple angles.

"That was a strange sight to see. It was pretty, but sort of scary. I'm not sure I could pull that off," Alize said timidly.

"Alchemy is a skill set that helps us understand each step of this process. I know how you feel, but I'm positive you can do this. As far as alchemy goes, this is the most basic of the basics. In cooking terms, it's like learning to use a kitchen knife. Getting further than this will depend on practice and talent, but anyone can do this with some training. Don't worry," Lorraine reassured her with a smile.

Someone with no mana would have been bewildered by what Lorraine just demonstrated, but she wasn't one to lie at times like these, so what she said must have been the truth.

I questioned whether I could do what Lorraine demonstrated as well, so I was glad she said that to Alize. I had more nimble fingers than most, but if and how that might be applicable to alchemy was a mystery. I could never handle mana that well either, but I had at least gotten more efficient at it over the last decade. Chances were it would be fine, but I was uncertain. My top priority was to not let Alize see me fail. I didn't know if Lorraine understood how I felt or not, but she moved on.

"Now why don't you two try it? Choose whatever materials you wish. All the goods Rentt collected are high quality, so anything should work."

Alize and I were unsure which materials to use, but we came to a decision after some time. I let Alize choose first, naturally. I gathered it all for her to begin with, so if I took the best goods before she had the chance, it would all be for nothing. I could live with the leftovers. Ultimately, I could collect more materials if I wanted to.

Alize selected wood from a birch shrub ent and the magic crystal from a mine goblin. I recommended using the magic crystal from a terra drake instead.

"This one is prettier, so I want this one," she said, picking up the mine goblin's magic crystal. It was a beautiful blue and was appealing to the eyes, but its quality was only middling. In contrast, the terra drake's crystal was bright red and of high quality. It was nothing compared to a tarasque's magic crystal, but out of what was available, the terra drake's was the best.

Lorraine seemed to pick up on my thoughts. "It's not like we're making the ultimate wand here. It's her first one, so let her make what she wants. She's more likely to succeed that way. There's no need to make her use something better," Lorraine said.

In that case, I supposed it was fine. The terra drake's magic crystal was my favorite of the bunch anyway, and I liked the ebony wood.

"Now that you've both picked your materials, it's time to paint a magic circle. Do you have brushes?" Lorraine asked.

We both did. Two ink bottles were sitting on the table too.

"Good. Then first of all, fill your brushes with mana. I did so earlier, but I'm sure you didn't notice. You don't need to use too much. If you overdo it, well, you just shouldn't, so I suppose I don't need to explain that. At any rate, pour mana into your brush little by little, then keep the mana steady as you dip the brush in the ink. Let's begin."

I did as described and filled the brush with a small amount of mana. I was used to this type of work by now, so it was a breeze. It was no different from adding mana to a weapon. Alize, however, had never done this before, so she was having some trouble.

A decade of experience made all the difference compared to a beginner, but Alize appeared to find that a bit frustrating.

"You won't beat me, Rentt!" she said and hyped herself up, but it was for nothing.

"Uh-oh, don't use too much mana," Lorraine cautioned.

"Huh?"

Alize poured tons of mana into her brush and dipped it in the ink, causing the black fluid to quiver and burst out of the bottle like a fountain. I grinned, garnering a glare from her pitch-black face.

I stifled a laugh and tried to act serious. "I see, so using too much mana will make the ink splatter. Better be careful," I said.

Lorraine nodded. "That's right, but don't fan the flames too much. And Alize, don't get worked up. I do think competition is good, but not for this particular work."

"Why?" Alize questioned. She didn't seem to understand, so Lorraine explained.

"I assume you've never applied mana to a brush before, but Rentt always uses mana on his weapon when he fights. He's been doing it for a decade. That means when it comes to this work, he's far from a novice."

"What the heck? No fair!" Alize cried out.

"What do you want? I can't go back to being a beginner now. This is my first attempt at alchemy, but controlling mana is a specialty of mine. I'd give up trying to outdo me at this, if I were you," I explained.

It should have been obvious anyway, but Alize sounded a bit discontented. Still, she was obedient and amiable enough. "I thought we'd learn how to do it together," she said. In other words, she hoped we would progress at the same pace. I knew where she was coming from.

"We can still do that, but there are some areas where I know what I'm doing, is all. Magic and alchemy aren't something you can use without learning them first."

"Are you sure, though?" Alize cocked her head, not entirely convinced.

"He's right," Lorraine said. "You're far better than Rentt a decade ago. If you're better than him in ten years, that means you win."

That was true, and I was sure she would leave me in the dust. I planned to keep getting stronger, but in a decade, Alize had the potential to become as strong as I was now.

"I'll do my best," Alize responded sincerely.

After that, Lorraine cast Linpio on her and brought out new ink so we could get back to work. It couldn't have been cheap, so I wondered just how much she had on hand, but it didn't matter.

I succeeded in applying mana to my brush on the first try, but it was a struggle for Alize. Even so, she got it right after about an hour. Her talent was worthy of envy. Learning this skill had taken me much longer. The mana within your body was easy enough to manipulate once you became aware of it, but expelling it from your body required some different sensibilities. I had managed to figure it out after around a week, nowhere near as fast as Alize.

"Then let's move on to painting the magic circle. You have to keep the mana in your brush, so this demands some concentration. Good luck," Lorraine said.

Alize and I got to work. Maintaining the mana in the brush was as natural to me as breathing, so I didn't need to focus that hard, but Alize was straining herself. She could do it, but her struggle showed she had some things left to learn. If she had reached my level in a single day, I would never have been able to show my face again.

Though if that did happen, it would only mean Alize's aptitude was phenomenal, so I couldn't complain.

"You did it already, Rentt?" Lorraine asked.

"Yeah, can you check if it's good or not?"

"I always knew you had good hands. You painted it perfectly. Speaking of which, are you a good artist too?"

"I don't know if I'd say I'm good. Average, maybe."

When I was out adventuring and had to describe the traits of monsters I encountered to other adventurers on the same job, I would draw on the ground to demonstrate. I got some practice from that. Having a variety of such experiences is what life is all about.

"Then you shouldn't have any problems. This is usable. Now let's see Alize's," Lorraine said and peered over at her side.

"How is it?" Alize asked.

"Not bad, but this part is a bit misshapen. It'll still work, but bigger mistakes can prevent the magic circle from working, or even produce unexpected effects. Try to be more careful," Lorraine warned her.

"What kind of unexpected effects?" Alize asked.

"There are all kinds, but a story commonly told among mages is about a mage named Conra who had no artistic talent. Conra was so gifted in the art of persuasion he became a court mage, but one day, he was put in charge of one of his country's rituals. That wasn't a problem in itself, but the ritual involved creating a magic circle that generated fireworks. Conra knew he was hopeless when it came to art, but he decided that if the magic circle failed, he would simply use magic to send fireworks into the air instead. But when he made the magic circle and triggered it, something dreadful happened. What do you think it was?"

"I don't know, what?"

"He summoned a fire dragon that burned the whole region to the ground."

The horrific conclusion turned Alize's face pale. The possibility that her magic circle could have similar results must have scared her.

"Well, this is just an old story we used to tell each other. Nothing so devastating will happen. Conra was bad at magic circles, but he was still an incredible mage with an immense quantity of mana. They say that's why his mistake was so catastrophic. Your mistakes might summon a little slime we could just stomp on, at the worst. That or it could make a loud sound or a weak explosion that wouldn't do any damage. You don't need to worry about it. I'll take care of anything that happens," Lorraine said, putting Alize at ease.

Even the process of pouring mana into the bronze board gave Alize a hard time. The object was different, but it was much the same as sending mana into the brush. That she would have difficulties with both was to be expected. It was the opposite case for me. Applying mana to weapons, brushes, or bronze boards was all identical, meaning my decade of experience putting a sliver of mana in my weapon at all times made this job simple.

I almost felt bad for Alize, but it's not like this came easy to me either. What she was attempting to accomplish in one day was something I had worked at for years. If anything, it was unfair that her skills were beginning to take shape so soon. Everything worked out when you had talent, but maybe my severe lack of talent was the real problem. Or maybe this was normal. I didn't know.

"All right, now place your magic crystal on the bronze board," Lorraine instructed after we finished painting our magic circles. "I shortened the process in my demonstration to save time, but it's too soon for you two to attempt that. You'll use the basic method and simply set the magic crystal on the board. Eventually, it will naturally absorb the magic circle."

Lorraine had done something to get the work over with right away, but it sounded like a difficult technique. I was interested in trying it, but Lorraine said it was too soon for us, so I doubted I could pull it off. I decided to accept taking the normal route with Alize.

If I were in a rush to learn alchemy, that would be another story, but I was a swordsman. Mastery of multiple skills could be convenient, but I wasn't so sure about alchemy. It wasn't a skill set that could get quick results for an adventurer. The ability to produce high-quality medicine on your own was valuable to be sure, but I had learned how to make medicine from the medicine woman in my hometown, albeit somewhat weaker medicine than that of an alchemist. If I found myself in real trouble beyond that, I could also access divinity.

I followed Lorraine's instructions and placed the magic crystal on the bronze board. The dried ink of the magic circle appeared to peel off and get sucked inside. It had happened in an instant for Lorraine, a flash of light and it was over, so I didn't get the chance to watch this part. It was an unusual sight now that I could see it in motion, but not too extraordinary. Lorraine nodded as she watched, implying the wand production was going smoothly so far. About ten minutes later, the final piece of the magic circle entered the magic crystal.

"All right, that's enough. Check to see if your magic circles entered properly," Lorraine suggested. We couldn't wait to look already, so right as Lorraine closed her mouth, we grabbed our crystals and peeked inside.

"Oh, I did it! It worked, Professor Lorraine!" Alize yelled. It sounded like hers turned out well.

"Let me see," Lorraine said and took the magic crystal so she could look inside. "Yes, it came out nicely. The magic circle is a little warped, but that shouldn't be an issue. A job well done for your first time, Alize." Lorraine patted Alize's head.

She shifted the discussion toward me. "So what about yours?"

"Well, uh…" I stammered. I didn't want to admit I felt ashamed, but I did. I could have sworn I followed Lorraine's directions though.

Lorraine looked at my odd behavior and furrowed her brow. "Rentt, what's with you?" she asked as she approached me, snatched my crystal, held it over her head, and peered inside.

"Can't you do anything normally? You know this is weird, right?" she asked and gave the magic crystal back.

I looked inside and saw a somewhat odd magic circle. I knew I had painted it on the bronze board with Lorraine's ink and it had entered the crystal. It should have been like when Lorraine did it, where the circle remained the same color once inside, but my crystal contained a magic circle that had a blotchy yellow and green pattern. It was honestly not a pleasant color.

"It's not pretty, I'll say that," I muttered.

"That's not the problem, but these things happen on occasion. If you have peculiar mana or a divine spirit's blessing, strange magic circles can appear in your magic tools. In your case, I think we know what the cause was," she claimed.

I knew what she was suggesting. I had divinity and the blessing of some divine spirit. My mana might have also been unusual due to my undead nature. Rather, after this, it was safe to say here was something off about my mana. I wondered if it was even possible for me to perform alchemy correctly.

I began to feel depressed. "This is bad, isn't it?" I asked Lorraine.

"No. It's a rare phenomenon, but it happens. Some people are born with abnormal mana, and there's no shortage of those with divine blessings. But any wand you make is going to have irregular properties. As long as you're prepared for that, there won't be a problem," she assured me.

That made it sound like there would still be a problem, but I could at least learn alchemy. That was good enough, but I didn't know what these irregular properties would be. That was the next question, but it couldn't be answered until the wand was finished.

"Show me your crystal," Alize asked while I was thinking, so I looked to Lorraine. I wanted to see if showing her something so bizarre would be bad for her education, but Lorraine nodded, so I handed the crystal to Alize.

"Wow, it's beautiful. Mine is an ordinary black magic circle. I'm kind of jealous," she said innocently.

It helped to hear that, though. I was keenly aware of how abnormal I was, but when even this simple thing came out wrong, it saddened me a bit. It was the type of depression I could get over in a couple days, but this was still a wretched, desolate reminder that I wasn't human. My lack of need for much sleep and my ability to recover from small wounds in a few seconds made me feel the same way.

But what Alize said blew those feelings away. What a wonderful disciple she was. I didn't know who was encouraging who. These thoughts occupied the depths of my heart as we continued making our wands. All that remained was the wand itself.

"Now it's time to shape your wands and combine them with your crystals. You're already mostly done, to be honest, but this is no way for a wand to look," Lorraine said.

"What does that mean?" Alize asked, cocking her head.

"Oh, magic catalysts are perfectly usable with nothing but a magic crystal. But attaching a grip makes the mana easier to control, not to mention it raises your mana amplification rate, so it's not just a matter of appearances, actually," Lorraine answered.

She went on to explain the reasons for grips further. "The wands we're making today won't work much differently than if you simply used a magic crystal, but more advanced catalysts will add other elements to the grip. For example, you can put materials inside or use multiple magic crystals that resonate with each other, among other things. The grip is like the foundation that holds your catalyst," she explained.

If a grip wasn't necessary, then magic crystals were able to function as catalysts by themselves. But grips could enhance magic catalysts. That raised some questions.

"Then are rings worse magic catalysts than wands and staffs?" Alize was quick to ask.

Setting multiple magic crystals on a ring would be a challenge. It was the logical conclusion, but Lorraine countered this.

"No, not necessarily. Well, wands and staffs are easier to make, but you can put multiple magic crystals on rings too. The ones you're using are big enough that it would be difficult, but monsters drop all kinds of magic crystals. Some are small enough that several could fit on a ring. If you use those, there's no issue."

"But couldn't you place a ton of small crystals on a staff, then?" Alize questioned.

"That's true, but there's a limit to how many magic crystals a catalyst can hold, regardless of the amount of space. Most use one, but you can use two if you're good. A quality piece of work might use three, and some unbelievably powerful ones use four. You can find catalysts with even more than that in some dungeons. A Legendary-class artisan could surpass these limits, but most alchemists can only reach three no matter how hard they try. If you can make a stable catalyst with four crystals, that's a skill you could make a living on. Want to try it?"

I would have called that unreasonable, but I strove for goals that seemed absurd from an outside perspective, so I wasn't one to talk. Alize seemed to have the same impression, but she was curious about something.

"Professor Lorraine, how many crystals can you use when you make catalysts?"

"Me? It's a secret. I can use at least three though, I'll tell you that much."

That seemed to imply she could make one with four crystals, too, but she didn't confirm either way. Knowing Lorraine, she would have said this whether she could do better than three or not.

Alize was about to ask something else, but Lorraine interrupted with, "Come on, let's get back to work. Making the grip isn't easy, so you'll have to focus." Alize never got to ask her question, but she seemed content enough. From her perspective, Lorraine was an amazing woman, so whether she could use three or four crystals wouldn't change much in her eyes. I saw Lorraine the same way.

At Lorraine's urging, I went back to my shrub ent wood. The wood was in the same state as when I collected it, so it was more or less a log.

"Pour mana into the surface," Lorraine said. "Then control the mana to only peel off that part and continue until you reach the proper size. You're working with fairly large materials, so you can make plenty of mistakes. Just try it."

Alize and I nodded and got to work. As expected, I had no trouble peeling away only what was necessary. Alize struggled, sometimes chopping off small slivers, sometimes cutting in a curved line, and sometimes removing nothing but bark. But in the end, she still managed to shave off only what was necessary. As impressive as ever.

"All right, now to shape your wood into a wand. This is basically the same. Use mana to compress and round the wood. But you're likely to fail the first attempt, Alize, so start by practicing on the pieces of wood you cut off. Once you get used to it, you can try the real deal. Okay?" Lorraine asked. Alize nodded.

I looked at Lorraine to see if I should do the same. Her expression implied that I ought to decide for myself. I had been quick to finish everything thus far, so she made Alize her priority instead. It was the right decision. I preferred to try things for myself anyway.

I'd heard how to do it, so that just left some trial and error. The problem was I needed the material I had just stripped down, so I carved some excess wood of the same size and used that to practice shaping a wand. I tried a few approaches. It felt somewhat like playing with clay. I could practice by making more than just a wand, so I used my mana to shape something else.

"Hey, look at this. Pretty good, eh?" I said to Alize and Lorraine. They looked at my handiwork with shock.

"Rentt, nice work. I had a rough enough time just making a wand," Alize said, holding a piece of wood shaped into a wand. Apparently she managed.

"Even I couldn't do that. Maybe you could sell these if you picked different models," Lorraine remarked.

Lorraine and Alize's eyes were glued to wooden figures of the two of them. I even had them pose. Lorraine was holding a staff and casting magic in a cool fashion. Alize was kneeling and praying to god as if she were at the Church of the Eastern Sky. She was pure and solemn. I was satisfied with how they came out.

"Take this lesson seriously. I'm confiscating these," Lorraine said and took them away. "Alize, you can have this one." She handed Alize the one modeled after her.

I was miffed about that because of all the work I put into them, but I couldn't complain after I ignored the assigned work during a class. I could have pointed out that this was a form of practice and relevant to the work at hand, but Lorraine would only see it as fooling around. If I could do this, I should have gone ahead and made the wand, as far as she was concerned. And she was absolutely right. I did screw around a bit. I felt bad about it, so I quickly shaped the wand.

"What next?" I asked brightly. Lorraine gave me an appalled look, but she soon got over it.

"Fine, this is the final step: combining your crystal with your wand. Do your best. You're almost there."

"Put them together like I demonstrated. I shouldn't have to explain this part," Lorraine said.

"Wait a second. You used mana to shift the tip of the wand around the crystal and hold it in place, I got that much, but what were those sparks about?" I interjected.

Lorraine laughed. "Well, good question. I was only kidding," she replied. "That part is important. I did everything at once during the demonstration, but combining your crystal and wand has a number of steps. You'll do that after this. First, you need to send a line through the wand."

"What do you mean by that?" Alize asked.

"Just what it sounds like. You create a path for mana to run through your wand. Mana can actually pass through regardless, but this makes it more efficient. This involves uniting the numerous winding mana paths that already exist in your wand into a single large, straight passage."

I understood what she was saying for the most part, but I had no idea how to do it. Alize must have felt the same way because she looked puzzled.

"How does that work?" she asked.

"It's rather abstract, but when you actually try it, you'll see it's not that hard. It's similar to how you shaped the wand. Start from the bottom of the wand, then slowly send you mana upward, focusing on the way it flows," she instructed.

Alize and I obeyed. I felt the mana separate as it ascended through the wand. Like water flowing through numerous branching paths, it traveled in different directions. I saw what Lorraine meant by this being inefficient. Alize seemed to understand as well.

"Are these the lines?" she asked Lorraine.

"Yes, but as I'm sure you've noticed, simply shaping your material into a wand caused the lines to stretch out and curve at random. If you make a wand like this, it won't be much better than a stick. We avoid that by taking those chaotic lines and straightening them out. This is done the same way you shaped the wand, by having your mana flow from one end of the wand to the other as you move the lines together. Can you do it?"

I didn't know if I could, but now I knew the method. Alize and I nodded and got to work, finding that Lorraine was right in that it was mostly identical to the previous step. The act of moving lines that were hidden inside the wand seemed to raise the difficulty a degree, but it involved largely the same kind of work. The difference was the lines in the wand all went in different directions. It felt like scooping every bit of scum from the surface of some soup.

That said, I enjoyed simple, repetitive work. When I was still human, I would go to the Water Moon Dungeon every day to hunt the same monsters until I tired myself out. This work was tolerable, and even fun, but Alize looked frustrated. She was young, so that was typical.

"Are you getting fed up?" Lorraine asked, startling Alize.

"Oh, no, um…" she stammered with shame. Lorraine laughed at her.

"I know how you feel from the first time I made a wand. I even threw my wand right at my teacher's face," Lorraine said, sharing a shocking memory.

"At their face, really?" Alize murmured, doubting she could ever do the same.

"Well, that's how tedious the work was, but it has a strong influence on the quality of your wand. Be patient and do the best you can."

"Okay!" Alize answered with energy and returned to work. This time she kept calm and immersed herself in the task.

I, on the other hand, was wondering something after that bit of encouragement.

"So what did that teacher do after that?" I asked Lorraine.

"Went into a furious rage. It was so terrifying I'd rather not remember it," she whispered in my ear. Then she shuddered.

I wondered what kind of teacher could make Lorraine say that, but much like me, Lorraine didn't talk about her history from before she had come to Maalt. I decided not to ask more questions. After that, Alize and I finished forming our lines.

"All right, good," Lorraine said after sending mana through our wands to check them. "You both did well for your first time. Alize, you straightened your lines as instructed, and Rentt, you're always so good at detailed work that it's sickening. There's no room for criticism."

"Let me see Rentt's wand!" Alize demanded out of curiosity. She borrowed my wand and sent mana through it. "Wow, what the? It's nothing like mine," she said with an astounded look.

"Well, it may feel that way, but don't let it get you down," Lorraine said to cheer her up. "You should have known from those wood figures he made that Rentt is abnormally dexterous. I can't do anything like that either. Even forming lines this meticulously is a challenge."

"It's hard for you too, Professor?" Alize said with shock.

"I wouldn't say hard, but certainly tedious. You might realize this after trying it, but this is something you could do nearly perfectly with enough patience. But not so much in this short a time.

"At any rate, that's enough of that. Next is the final step, combining the crystal and the wand. This is a bit difficult. You have to handle your mana differently in one hand than the other. One hand sends mana into the crystal while the other does the same for the wand, but it doesn't matter which hand is which. If you fill the lines in your wand with enough mana, light will burst from the tip of the wand like you saw in my demonstration. You do the same with the crystal, but because you didn't mess with the lines in that, light will emit from the entire thing until it nears the tip of the wand, at which point the light will be drawn to that. Don't mind it too much. Also, I had both the wand and the crystal levitate as I did it, but that's a relatively advanced technique, so you two should do it by hand," Lorraine instructed.

We picked up our wands and crystals and began filling them with mana.

Half a minute after I began pouring mana into my wand, sparks flew from its tip. "Lorraine, is this good?" I asked.

"Yes, that's fine, but you also need to fill the magic crystal with mana until it looks like I demonstrated. Keep the wand like it is. Can you do it?"

"Well, it shouldn't be too difficult."

Each hand had to perform a different task, making it too challenging for some to manage. With that in mind, Alize was performing well. She was a bit behind me, but she kept her wand glowing as she charged her magic crystal with mana. I might have been biased, but she was remarkably adept.

"You may have realized this now that you've tried it out, but magic crystals require more mana, otherwise you end up in the annoying position you're in now. Next time you make a catalyst, try keeping that in mind," Lorraine suggested.

"I see," I said with a nod. Alize was focused on distributing her mana, so she had no time to respond. Doing this was like trying to juggle with one hand while writing a letter with the other. Adding a third task to that list would be difficult, so Alize's silence was understandable.

"Oh, my magic crystal looks good," I remarked. At last, it began to glow as well. The light from the wand shone in only one direction, but the light from the crystal traveled everywhere. Lorraine said this was normal, so I had to assume it was.

Lorraine looked at my progress. "You can move on to the next step, Rentt. Bring your crystal and your wand close together," she instructed.

When I did, the light from the crystal directed itself toward the wand. "Do I just stick them together?" I asked.

"It's not like you're using glue. Reshape the tip of the wand around the crystal to hold it in place. However, you have to do this without ruining the lines inside the wand. This is fairly challenging, so be careful."

"Does it matter what shape I make it?"

"No, and many people get creative with this part. I wouldn't recommend getting too fancy with your first attempt, though, but—"

"Professor!" Alize shouted. Her crystal had also started to emit light.

"Anyway, you can figure things out yourself," Lorraine said and turned to guide Alize.

I focused on my own work, unsure what shape to make the tip of my wand. I did recall seeing some in shops with different decorations. If you had to shape the tip a certain way, then those presumably wouldn't exist, but I didn't know how far I could go without ruining my work. I started off simple and made steady changes, learning I could make huge alterations without an issue. There did seem to be a limit, though; I got the sense that too much movement would break the lines. It was like bending a stick until near snapping. If you were lucky, a little more bending might curve the stick a bit more, but in most cases it would break. Regardless, it was malleable enough to leave plenty of options. With that thought, I immersed myself in forming the tip of my wand.

"All right, you're done. Good work, Alize," I heard Lorraine say, so I looked over. Alize was gripping her finished wand. The magic crystal was fixed in place, and I now sensed the stable mana of a magic item.

"So this is my wand," Alize said and stared at the stick with glee. She seemed tired, judging by her sweaty forehead and heavy panting.

"Now you can try casting spells with it. You too, Rentt. Are you done yet?" Lorraine said and looked toward me. Her eyes opened wide with shock. "Again?"

"What?" I asked. I had finished around the same time as Alize. I'd reached the last step sooner, but I spent more time on the wand's tip.

She pointed at my wand. "That. The tip of your wand. That's some impressive work," she muttered.

Curious, Alize popped out from behind Lorraine and peered at my wand. "Wow, what the? It's so detailed," she said, startled.

Lorraine picked up my wand and looked at it from different angles. "The dragon's holding the crystal in its mouth. This is an incredibly detailed sculpture of a dragon. These sorts of decorations usually aren't made with mana manipulation alone, you know," Lorraine pointed out.

Specifically, this was the dragon that had eaten me. At the time, I thought my life was over, so its appearance was so ingrained it was the first thing that came to mind. To be honest, I did think it was kind of gauche. Lorraine seemed to agree because she looked at me like I was crazy for picking the creature that had devoured me. But that wasn't something we could discuss while Alize was around, so I asked something else that was on my mind.

"How do you shape the tip of a wand other than mana manipulation, then?"

"Oh, decorations like that are usually made while you're shaping the material into a wand to begin with. People tend to make the tip larger and then shave it down into the shape they want."

"Why go through that much trouble?" I asked. Mana manipulation felt like it provided more freedom with the shape. I assumed it was because something like this required obsessive focus, so it took a while.

Lorraine held her head in her hands. "You can get by with mana manipulation to a certain extent, but this much detail isn't normally possible. Unless you happen to be an expert at controlling mana, carving it by hand with tools specifically for the job will give you better results. But I guess the rules don't apply to you," she complained.

"So Rentt's really special?" Alize asked.

"Well, that's one way to put it. Of course, a top-class artisan could do this kind of work too, but Rentt's never even done this before. I always thought he was dexterous, but now that I'm seeing him work in my field of expertise, I'm reminded of that all over again," Lorraine said.

"I guess I should be sorry," I said, apologizing.

"You've got nothing to be sorry about. In fact, this is magnificent. Next time I make a wand, I'll let you handle the tip. If I did that, then I could..." Lorraine lowered her head and began whispering to herself before looking back up. "Well, in any case, your wands are finished. They both came out well enough. Now you can try them and see how well they work as catalysts."

"Okay!" Alize shouted, covering up Lorraine's suspicious whispering.

It was time to see the wand in action. I was about to cast a spell right then and there, but Lorraine stopped me. "Don't try it in my house. Let's go outside," she requested in a surprising display of common sense.

We headed out, but we only went as far as some empty ground on the outskirts of town.

"Now you can cause all the explosions you want, and nobody will complain," Lorraine said.

Despite her reassurance, I couldn't imagine the owner of the land being okay with that. And though it was a large space, there were houses visible in the distance. Maybe nobody would notice an explosion, but I wasn't so sure.

"Wouldn't the owner of this place be unhappy about that?" I asked Lorraine.

"No, I wouldn't be. This is my land."

"Huh?" I blurted out. It was an unexpected response, but it explained why Lorraine wasn't worried. If this was her land, then we could do anything we wanted. Unless we opened a doorway to Hell and let tons of demons through to attack the city. That would be a huge problem, but I didn't anticipate anything that serious. Although mages in legends and fables tended to make those mistakes, I didn't even know how that would be done.

"I perform some experiments I'd rather not do at home, you see. That's why I bought this land a while back. We're far enough from the center of town that it wasn't too expensive despite the size," Lorraine explained.

Despite what she said, the land was still too vast to be that cheap. I knew Lorraine was rich, though. She had always had a mysterious source of wealth. Buying a house was nothing to her either, so it wasn't that great a surprise.

At any rate, if this was true, then there was no need for concern. However, I wondered if this was so precarious it had to be done outside.

"Hey, can your first wand really be that dangerous?" I asked Lorraine.

"Not usually. Depending on the spell you use, most beginners can cast elementary spells in the home without a hitch. In your case, though, I'm a bit uneasy. You're good enough at mana manipulation that I don't think it'll be that bad, but you can't be too careful. Also, Alize has a lot of mana herself, so she might find it hard to keep it under control. I don't want you to worry about that while you test your magic, so I figured this would be the best place."

If more mana meant it was harder to control, then maybe it felt different casting magic with a wand than without one, considering catalysts were for stabilizing and amplifying your mana. Stabilization was one thing, but amplification could be a hindrance. Losing control as a result was probably the reason for Lorraine's concern.

"Well, whatever the case, give it a try. I've only taught you basic magic, so that's what you'll have to go with. It'll be the easiest way to understand the power of your wand anyway," Lorraine said.

Alize and I nodded.

"Alize, why don't you go first? Remember your incantations?"

"Yes, I'll be fine!"

"Good answer. Then Rentt and I will stand back a bit. Go when I say we're ready."

"Okay!"

We walked a short distance away, and Lorraine yelled to Alize that she could start.

"Fire, use my mana as your fuel and manifest before me: Aliumage!" she chanted. The mana within Alize condensed and flowed to her wand. The energy swelled until flames burst from the tip. They were fiercer than I expected, to the point I questioned whether this was elementary magic. In my past experiences with this spell, the fire only burned from the fingertip, but this was more like the flames from a torch.

"What? What is this?" Alize stammered, intimidated by the size of the flame.

Lorraine approached and cast a spell to make the fire disappear, much to Alize's relief. I walked up to her too.

"That was awesome, Alize. I didn't know you could make such big flames with basic magic," I said, complimenting her.

"I wasn't expecting that either," she replied. She was still a bit tense.

Lorraine overheard us and butted in. "It sounds like you have the wrong idea. You don't typically get flames that large, but like I said, Alize has a lot of mana. That's why they were so big. Most beginners wouldn't be able to do this without a wand, regardless of how much mana they had, but the wand changes everything. It helps you control your magic and use it more efficiently. This isn't all good, though," she said.

"What's bad about it?" Alize asked, curious.

"If you rely on your wand too much, then one day you won't be able to control your mana without it. You could also become unable to move your mana without a wand."

"Is that a big problem?"

"Yes, a fatal one, you could say. You'd have to be in contact with your wand at all times to be able to fight as a mage. But young people these days choose to depend entirely on their wands for magic anyway. It's a much easier way to go about it. They start right off training with their wands, getting just good enough with it to go off adventuring. It's pitiful," she said as if she weren't also young.

I was going to joke about that, but she seemed serious, so I decided against it. She was past the average marrying age, so maybe you could say she wasn't that young. I was about the same age, though, just a little older. But when it came to our mental ages, people often thought I was younger.

"But I see mages around Maalt using magic without a wand all the time," Alize pointed out.

Lorraine nodded. "Yes, I see them levitating their purchases on the way home from shopping sometimes. The first time I saw that, I found it surprising as well. You don't see things like that in the Empire anymore, so it had been a while," Lorraine said, referring to her homeland, the Lelmudan Empire. They were supposed to be an advanced civilization with great progress in the field of magic, but maybe when it came to magic without a wand, that was somewhat in question.

"How did the Empire end up that way?" I asked.

"I just mentioned the disadvantages of wands, but there are advantages too. Detailed work is far easier with wands than without, as is larger scale work. The Empire engages in a lot of research on magical weapons and tools, so their mages keep wands on hand at all times. When you use something often enough, you start to depend on it. Do that even longer and people start to feel training with wands from the start is more efficient. As a result, that's how thoughts have evolved in the Empire. Of course, some can still use magic without a wand, but they can never gain influence among the Empire's mages. That includes me," she explained.

That was the fate of something that became too convenient, I supposed. But what Lorraine said seemed to imply some circumstances behind why she left the Empire.

Lorraine changed her tone. "Well, enough about that. Let's focus on your wands for the time being. I may have a lot of criticisms, but they're still generally useful tools. Now, Rentt, it's your turn. Alize and I will stand back."

I nodded, ready to try out my new wand.

"Hey, aren't you a little too far away? Just what do you think I'm going to do?"

I couldn't help but ask. Lorraine said they would stand back, but now they looked like specks from my perspective. It was about ten times further than the distance we stood at when Alize practiced. I wondered if I had done something to intimidate them, but when I thought about it more, an undead vampire was probably worth fearing.

"We're ready, Rentt!" Lorraine shouted from afar. That meant I could use magic now, I guessed. At that distance, something insane would have to happen to bring them any harm, so maybe it was for the best.

I went with the same magic as Alize, a life spell called Aliumage. I knew what it should look like after watching Alize, so I figured it would be easy enough to pull off. Considering a wand could strengthen a mage's control and amplify their mana, there was no reason I would fail. All I had to do was manage the power of the spell, but I had to try it at least once to get a feel for it.

Honestly, this wasn't my first time using a wand. But that was back when I was alive and had next to no mana, so there wasn't much to amplify. A droplet multiplied several times was still only a few droplets. But now I clearly had more mana, so I could look forward to different results. With that in mind, I filled my body with mana, focused it into my hand, and poured the energy into the wand.

"Fire, use my mana as your fuel and manifest before me: Aliumage," I chanted, and fire spewed from the wand's tip. It felt like the wand vastly amplified my power, so I frantically withdrew some mana. Regardless, an intense blaze burned. Thankfully no buildings were around. Lorraine's decision to stand that far away turned out to be correct. I had been sure of my ability to control mana, but this incident made me less confident.

I needed a bit of practice with the wand, but I didn't panic in the face of the flames the way Alize had. That was the power of my extra 25 or so years of life. I stopped supplying the flame with mana and adjusted its direction as I stared at it for a few seconds. When I confirmed that the flames were gone, I waved to Lorraine and Alize.

"You can come over now!" I shouted.

They observed for a bit to see if that was true before they approached. They were cautious, but maybe that was necessary. Wands could trigger by accident, and if some mana had remained stored inside it somehow, it could cause some odd reactions. They wanted to see if that would happen.

"Your Aliumage was super big," Alize remarked.

"Good thing we stood all the way out there. We would've been burnt to a crisp otherwise," Lorraine said with a smile. In reality, she would probably have conjured up a barrier and saved them anyway, but mistakes could have occurred. She was right overall.

"But that was a little oversized for Aliumage. I know you have a lot of mana, but that spell shouldn't produce flames like that."

"Really? But you can't deny what you just saw," I pointed out.

"True. Hm, Rentt, try another spell. You know a water-based life spell called Mah, don't you?"

Mah generated a cup's worth of water. It was helpful for adventurers, and it was one of the few spells I could cast with what little mana I had. I got a sense of what Lorraine was thinking.

"Yeah. I see, so I should test whether it's the same for other elements?" I assumed.

Some people excelled at specific elements of magic. Most humans could use all spells equally, but some leaned heavily toward certain types. There were many theories as to why that was true. If you were born near a volcano, for example, then you might end up more proficient at fire magic. The blessing of a divine spirit could also give you the capacity to specialize in spells of that spirit's element.

I had been blessed by a plant-type spirit, so if anything, I felt I should have been bad with fire. But maybe it didn't work how

I expected. It was strange, but Lorraine must have thought I should determine just where my specialties lay.

I decided to test the Mah spell. Alize and Lorraine stood back again just in case. I was unsure whether that was necessary, but after what happened with the last spell, I couldn't blame them.

When I heard Lorraine give me the signal, I cast the spell. "Water, soak up my mana and condense before me: Mah."

All life spells had similar incantations. As basic magic, they were simple in their construction. However, that made them that much easier to mix up. That's why when Lorraine asked if I knew the spell, I wasn't perfectly confident.

I wasn't positive I said it right, but my mana focused into the wand, reassuring me. Then water appeared from the tip of the wand. It was a fairly large orb, but it was nothing compared to the ludicrous size of the flames I had conjured before. This was maybe a size larger than Alize's flames, but that was all.

I sustained it for a few seconds to watch it and then let it disappear. When they confirmed it was gone, Lorraine and Alize returned.

"I knew it. You may be abnormally good at fire magic," Lorraine said as she thought to herself.

Judging by the results, I had to agree. "Better than I am at water magic, at least. But now I want to know about the other elements," I said with curiosity.

"I'd like to test more too, but you can't test absolutely everything. Those are the only two spells you can use anyway, aren't they? You could likely use other elementary spells right away if I taught you the incantations, but even having you test life magic is terrifying. That's enough for today," Lorraine said and put a cap on things.

She was right about that. I had enough experience with those two spells to sustain them, but there was no telling if I could do the same with unfamiliar magic. I probably could, but if anything bad happened, it would already be too late. I didn't know my body that well, so it wouldn't hurt to be careful.

That day, I was contacted by the Stheno Company. When I asked the messenger what they wanted, I was told they had acquired a magic bag I could buy if I wanted it. If not, it would go up for auction. They wanted me to come as soon as possible, so I rushed to prepare and headed to the Stheno Company.

Magic bags were rare items. If you wanted one that could fit a few orcs or so, that wasn't too hard to find. But what I had asked of Sharl, the head of the Stheno Company, was a bag that could contain a tarasque. Those were hardly in circulation, and whenever one popped up, it sold right away. I was delighted that he had even bothered to contact me about it.

When I arrived at the Stheno Company, the employee who had shown me around last time took me to the reception room like before. I again took the elevator up. It never stopped being fascinating. I wondered if Lorraine could put one in her house, but maybe a home didn't need anything like this. The Stheno Company had to use all the connections at their disposal to get one in the first place, so if someone asked to get one in their home, they'd likely be turned down. Lorraine might try to make one herself if I brought it up, but I didn't want one that badly. Sadly, I had to give up on it. My dreams were shattered.

After I got off, I enjoyed some tea and snacks in the reception room as I waited. They had these little brown boards this time. I didn't realize they were food when I first saw them, but then the employee spoke up.

"That's chocolate, a new treat that's gaining popularity in the West. It can be solid or liquid depending on the temperature, so they serve it in all kinds of ways. It's delicious."

I had never heard of chocolate before, but it smelled sweet. That was enough to assume it tasted good, but it still looked like a little slab. I could fit the whole thing in my mouth, but I didn't know if I was supposed to.

"Do you just eat it like this?" I asked.

"Yes, of course."

I carefully stuck it in my mouth. The sweet flavor and a mild bitterness spread across my tongue. "It's good," I said with approval.

"Thank you," the employee said and left.

I took that time to have my fill of chocolate. I never knew such delicious sweets existed. Just as I was told, the chocolate melted from the heat in my mouth. It went pretty well with tea, too, but I thought it might go even better with some strong alcohol. But I certainly couldn't ask for booze here. It was good enough by itself either way.

I kept chowing down on the chocolate until I heard a knock at the door.

"It's Sharl. May I come in?"

I frantically looked at my fingers and noticed they were smeared with chocolate, so I pulled a cloth out of my magic bag to wipe them off. I figured my mouth wasn't that clean either and wiped that too. I had no way to check how much I got off, so I reshaped my mask to cover the lower half of my face.

"Yes, go ahead," I said with feigned calmness.

Sharl entered the room. "Good to see you again, Rentt. How have you been since then?"

His question was vague, but based on my relationship with him, only one topic came to mind. Sharl must have meant what happened with Nive and the saint. He wanted to know if I'd had any problems with them since we last met.

I shook my head. "I think it's been fine for the most part, but maybe I just haven't noticed anything," I replied.

I wouldn't be surprised if Nive had some stealth skills. Actually, there was a 100% chance that was true, given the absurd number of vampires she had killed. But I hadn't done anything suspicious since we last met. Or at the very least, nothing that would pin me down as a vampire. I even stopped going out late at night unless absolutely necessary. True, my magic training from earlier had surprising results, but it was nothing that abnormal. My most incriminating activity was I went around buying assorted items for my journey, but travel wasn't uncommon, so that shouldn't have been a problem. I assumed I was fine.

"That's good," Sharl said. "After all the trouble you were put through, I was eager to know how business has been for you since then."

He was far busier than the average man, and not in any position to give a single adventurer his time, so I had wondered why he wanted to see me again. But his explanation made sense. Still, I didn't think he needed to go out of his way. Maybe he was just affable, but Sharl hadn't known the details about Nive's suspicions of me in the first place. My guess was Nive wanted to capture and destroy vampires as quickly and subtly as possible, hence her secrecy. That was annoying for me, as her target, but vampires did tend to hide within crowds.

If she had cause to suspect someone, then confirming her suspicions was the natural course of action.

"You don't need to worry, all her suspicions were cleared up. And I hear you even got a magic bag for me," I said.

"Oh, that's right. I'll have it brought out right now," Sharl replied and rang the bell on the table. The employee came in carrying a silver tray holding a shabby bag, set it on the table, and left.

"Is this it?"

"Yes, a 1,800-gold coin magic bag, just as you asked. Or so I'd like to say, but…" Sharl trailed off.

"Is this not that?" I asked, worried.

"Not quite, no, but that doesn't mean this is a poor-quality bag. The opposite, actually. These go for anywhere from 2,000 to 2,500 gold coins."

That sounded like a big difference to me. Not that I minded a better product, but I would have appreciated a thought about my wallet. 1,800 gold coins was 18 platinum coins, and that was expensive as it was. I could pay up to 20 platinum coins with the compensation I got from Nive, but I didn't know about anything more than that.

My concern must have been obvious, because Sharl laughed. "No, I don't expect you to pay 2,000 coins. Rather, I'm greatly indebted to you, so I'll sell this to you for 1,800 and we'll call it even. How does that sound?"

It wasn't a bad deal for me, of course, but I didn't know why he lowered the price so much. I understood Sharl felt like he owed me, but that was a big sum of money.

Sharl seemed to know what I was thinking. "Well, I won't claim I have no ulterior motives, but I promise I'm not plotting anything," he said.

I cocked my head. "What does that mean?"

"First of all, if I give you this great deal, we can put the past behind us going forward, right?"

He responded honestly, and I had to say he was probably right. Some might have wanted to cut ties with him after what happened, but I didn't feel the need to go that far. It was all Nive's fault anyway. And any other company would likely take Nive's request the same way. The support for the Church of Lobelia was just that powerful, though that support seemed more like something Nive was dragging around.

"That's true, I suppose we can for the most part," I answered. I still felt cautious around him, but if we cut ties, I would lose access to information. That would only be more frustrating.

"For the most part, eh? Understood, I see you aren't too trusting. Then secondly, and you can laugh at this if you want, but as a merchant, I suspect you might have some value to me," he admitted.

This sounded like the real reason for his offer, given the intensity in his voice, but I didn't know what he was implying. Maybe I had some value as a vampire, but I didn't think that was it. He meant it in a more abstract sense.

"I don't think I have anything to offer in particular, though," I said.

"Really? Then maybe my judgment is off, but I wouldn't think so. Besides, you're going to be a Mithril-class adventurer one day, aren't you? If that comes to pass, then it'll surely be worth staying connected with you. In other words, this is an investment of sorts," he added, recalling what I had told him in passing. I meant what I said, but I didn't think he took me seriously. Apparently he did.

"I hope to reach my goal, but a lot of people say how difficult it is."

"I would believe it. Most Bronze-class adventurers never reach Mithril-class in their wildest dreams, but you'll never make it if you don't try. I started off with a modest store myself, but now I have this whole company. Anything is possible," Sharl said.

I never knew he was such a sympathetic person. "You accomplished that without any inheritance or anything?" I asked.

"That wouldn't be quite accurate. My father ran a store, but it was a tiny general store. I was the one who expanded it. I always said one day our store would be the biggest business in the kingdom, back when it was still only a dream."

This was the reason Sharl didn't make fun of my ambitions when I mentioned them. As for Nive, I didn't know what she was thinking. I doubted making fun of me was even on her mind. Saint Myullias was, of course, a saint, so she wouldn't belittle someone for their dreams. Not that being a saint guaranteed a positive personality, but most of those who belonged to a religious organization tried to keep up appearances.

"That sounds like a lot to invest in a dreamer, though," I said. Selling something that went for up to 2,500 gold coins for a mere 1,800 meant a 700-gold-coin loss. That would be enough to eat shish kebabs from street vendors every day for the rest of my life. Or it would be if I weren't already dead. In any case, it was a lot of money, and yet he was willing to give it up.

"Maybe this is a lot of money to you, but it's not much to my company. Besides, I know your financial situation. Twenty platinum coins is the most I could wring out of you. Magic bags are hard enough to come by as it is, too. I tried to get an 1,800-gold-coin bag like you requested, but none appeared on the market.

This is what I managed to find, and I do hate to have to lower the price, as any merchant would, but…"

It was true magic bags were hard to obtain. The only means an ordinary adventurer had of obtaining one was to ask someone who already had one or to find one at an auction or in a dungeon. Even then, few people would give up their magic bags. They were seldom spotted in dungeons, so auctions were the best bet.

Maybe that was no different for a merchant. There were craftsmen who made magic bags, but nobody knew who they were, and gigantic companies kept nearly all of them to themselves. The Stheno Company might have been big compared to most in Yaaran, but they still didn't have that many craftsmen or connections. Their only options were to search the auctions, check other businesses, or buy them off adventurers who happened to find one. That would make it hard to obtain one of a specific size. However, it hadn't taken long for Sharl to get one that was close enough. That was a great accomplishment, excepting that I couldn't afford it at full price. I could see why Sharl hated to sell it at a loss.

"So what'll it be? Will you buy it?" he asked.

It was a difficult decision, but I might never have the chance to acquire one of these again. I still didn't fully trust him, but this was just an ordinary transaction. There was no reason to expect him to make some unreasonable demand after I bought it. But even with all that, I couldn't answer.

"Oh, that reminds me, this magic bag has a special function. It can change its appearance," Sharl said and picked up the bag. He focused on it, and it took the form of a leather bag. Then a knapsack. Then a box. "This is one reason for the price. The storage space by itself would only put it in the 2,000-coin range," he continued.

I had heard of items like this, but I'd never seen one before. Craftsmen's products had a fixed appearance, so this must have been found in a dungeon. For Sharl to have obtained this so soon, he had to have been on the lookout.

Now that I saw what the bag could do, I couldn't contain my desire for it. I was almost set on buying it anyway, so this just sealed the deal.

"I'll take it. Here, 18 platinum coins," I said and stacked the coins on the table.

Maybe that was a waste of money. The thought occurred to me as I left the Stheno Company with the bag, but I soon shook my head. I needed this to begin with, and it was worth more than I paid for it. Even if I hadn't bought this one now, I would still need one someday, so picking it up while I knew I could was the right choice. I could also use it to make the same amount of money I had paid. I could always take down another tarasque, or hunt all the orcs I could find. Either way, I would make gold coins by the hundreds.

But I was kind of forgetting how to handle money. Bronze-class adventurers never made huge purchases like this. I could only afford to because of my unique body, so I had to be thankful for that. I did want to become human again, but at the same time, I didn't. It was a peculiar position to be in.

With that important business taken care of, I had another objective. Before I left on my journey, there was a problem I wanted to solve. My appearance had made it impossible to fix previously, but now I could at least pass for a human. There was likely no way to confirm I wasn't one, as Nive proved, so I thought now was the time.

The matter at hand was my position at the adventurer's guild. It had yet to become an issue, but if someone like Nive caught wind of me again, it could get ugly. If possible, I wanted to get them to register "Rentt Faina" and "Rentt Vivie" as the same person by negotiating with Maalt's guildmaster. It was a dangerous gamble, but I had a chance. The guild was by no means a squeaky clean organization, as I knew well.

It would probably work out, I thought to myself as I set foot inside the guild.

Chapter 3: Existence and Status

"Rentt? What brings you here today?"

Sheila looked up from the reception desk and watched curiously as I approached. Her confusion must have been due to the hour of my arrival. Nobody took requests this late. You couldn't collect rewards for finished jobs at this time either, so she couldn't guess why I was there.

"Well, I have some business to attend to. Can you get ahold of the guildmaster for me? I want to talk to him."

Sheila was surprised. "Rentt, are you all right? When you came in here, I more or less imagined that was why, but the guildmaster's not that forgiving," she warned, putting the pieces together.

There were only so many reasons why I would go out of my way to see the guildmaster. The most important of them regarded my current registration status, and that was the cause for her concern.

"I know, but it's not like I've done anything wrong. I'm sure he's willing to hear me out," I argued.

"I think you've done plenty worth criticizing," Sheila said, her tone doubtful.

Double registration wasn't that severe of a crime, but I couldn't argue that it wasn't a crime at all. She was right in that sense. Still, it wasn't a massive sin, so I could try to rectify it. Maybe there was some need for caution, but I didn't think it was that serious.

"A lot of people do bad things. Anyway, let me talk to the guildmaster," I repeated.

Sheila looked uneasy for a moment. "If you insist, then I'm sure there won't be a problem. This way, please," she said and stood up.

We stopped at a door, and Sheila knocked on it twice.

"Guildmaster, it's me, Sheila Ibarss. Rentt Vivie the Bronze-class adventurer would like to speak with you. He's here with me now."

A deep, crude voice answered, but it was hesitant. "Rentt Vivie the Bronze-class adventurer? All right, let him in."

Sheila was startled by the response. "As you wish," she replied and then opened the door. She prompted me to step inside, but she didn't come in with me. Instead, she closed the door behind me. I heard her walk away, presumably back to her work station.

Inside the room was a man at a desk. I knew right away that this was the guildmaster. Most guildmasters worked their way up from staff positions at the guild. It was a desk job for the most part, but the intimidating aura this man exuded didn't belong to someone who did paperwork. His arms looked about as burly as a rough and rowdy adventurer's, if not more so, and he had a scar that ran down the middle of his left eye. Loose clothes hid his body, but I could tell he was huge. His right eye glowered at me like that of a warrior.

His rough appearance was to be expected; he used to be an adventurer. He had retired due to injuries, but before he could go back to his hometown, Yaaran's grand guildmaster had appointed him as Maalt's guildmaster. That was quite unusual. Retiring from adventuring to work at a guild was common enough, but becoming a guildmaster right away was one sizable promotion. Many had been opposed to this, and I'd heard there had been a lot of chaos at Maalt's guild after it happened, but it had settled by the time I became an adventurer. Now the guild was in a far better state than those in most other cities.

"Hm, you, eh? Oh, I ought to introduce myself first. I'm the guildmaster of the Maalt guild, Wolf Hermann. Good to meet you, Bronze-class adventurer Rentt Vivie," he said.

There was something strange about the way he emphasized his words.

I was afraid of getting punched before I even said anything. The way he said, "Good to meet you," sounded almost sarcastic. There could only be one reason why: this wasn't our first meeting. Now the question was how much did he know? I had to guess he knew a lot. As long as I was living in this town, information would find its way to the guild one way or another. Not to mention both my history as Rentt Faina and my work as Rentt Vivie were recorded and available here. If he took the time to think about it, there was enough evidence to presume Rentt Faina and Rentt Vivie were one and the same. If anything, it was odd that I hadn't been exposed before now.

Not that I was anyone important. There was no reason anyone beyond my old friends, to whom I had already explained almost everything, should care about my situation. That only left those distant acquaintances I couldn't even call friends, but they knew all about the darker side of adventuring. If they didn't see you around, then most would assume you were dead. It was too painful to speak of the dead, so they tended to go unmentioned. These sorts of incidents happened. I couldn't imagine anyone cared to get to the bottom of what had happened to me.

That said, usually some rumors did spread around, but I had yet to hear anything about my own death. That meant someone was keeping that information concealed. I had a guess as to who it was, but that was all an assumption.

I decided to act like I didn't notice anything. Maybe I could dance around it while I figured this out.

"Right, nice to meet you, Guildmaster. I'm Rentt Vivie, a Bronze-class adventurer. I know this was sudden, so I appreciate you taking the time to talk to me."

Guildmaster Wolf looked fed up already. "Yeah whatever, that's enough of that. I hate when my time's wasted, Rentt Faina. I know why you're here. This is about your double registration? I'll do something about that for you, just tell me all about it," he declared, defying all expectations.

I gulped. "I have no clue what you're talking about."

"I said drop it. But I guess you're not getting the picture. I get it, we've barely met each other, let alone spoken much. But I've had my eye on you for a long time, you know that?"

I hadn't known that in the past, but I did by now. Rather, I had realized it to some extent before. He had jokingly asked a few times if I would work for the guild. I never thought he was serious, but I'd since heard from Sheila that he was. Though I didn't know what he saw in me, it was certain he had his eye on me. Still, I wondered what that had to do with anything.

"When I heard you disappeared, I'll be straight with you, I was the most shocked of anyone. Why, you ask? You see, I was so sure that any time now you'd quit the adventurer life and come work for the guild. But then you up and vanished, and judging from the way it happened, I thought you were dead. That's how it goes with adventurers. We all know it happens. But still, I was just stunned. You could've made my job a lot easier, really lowered the death rate for adventurers around here, but then I lost you," Wolf explained.

I had no intention of giving up on adventuring. I'd spent close to ten years without a serious accomplishment, so I could see where he got that idea, but I was too tenacious to give up like that.

Wolf seemed to see what I was thinking. "Well, maybe you never would've given up while you were healthy, but the older you are, the slower you get. One day you would take a blow you couldn't recover from. No way you could keep up adventuring then, so you'd need another job. I thought you'd want something as close to adventurers as possible, so if you got an offer from the guild, you'd take it. What do you think?"

I wasn't so sure. If I were injured so badly I couldn't keep adventuring, then maybe that would be my only choice. I would likely want to do something close to adventuring too. That's how much I loved my work.

"Wondering why I think that?" Wolf asked. "Because the same thing happened to me. Just look at this eye. I can't go out adventuring nowadays, but I can at least raise the next generation of adventurers. Never expected the guild to hire me, but life's full of surprises. And adventurers like working for an ex-adventurer a lot more than for some snob who doesn't know anything. Pretty sure Yaaran's grand guildmaster is an ex-adventurer too, so I think that was the idea. Especially for this guild out here in the sticks. And, I was thinking I'd do the same thing for you."

What he said made sense, but I still wanted to know why me in particular. Guildmasters seldom bothered to check information on Bronze-class adventurers. There were hundreds of us, and the job of guildmaster didn't permit that kind of time.

"I'd been watching you for a while, and when I got a report on the Bronze-class exam, something stood out to me. Now, sometimes people do pass on their first try, that's fine. But it was the way you passed it, Rentt. You avoided every trap. Not exactly something a newbie can do. You'd either need a lot of experience, or a lot of skill. So I checked your name, and Rentt Vivie reminded me an awful lot of this other adventurer who drew my eye, Rentt Faina. You see what I'm saying?"

Wolf's explanation was easy to understand. Given the circumstances, I could see how he had realized who I was so early. I didn't take much care to hide my identity, so that was the biggest reason. If I'd wanted to fully hide away, I would have picked a more distinct name and chosen a different town to operate in after I got my adventurer's license. I knew too many people in this town to conceal myself completely. I figured as much, which is why I let my friends know who I was. Even when it came to the guild, I knew I might have to talk about my double registration eventually. If I wanted to be convincing once it came to that, I needed it to be clear enough who I was.

I didn't have a strong idea what Guildmaster Wolf was like, but I knew Maalt's guild engaged in less fraud and collusion than others. It had a lower death rate for adventurers too. Also, the impression I got from our few conversations told me he could be reasoned with. I felt that as long as I was honest, he would hear me out.

It might have been a gamble to be so open with my identity, but it paid off because he picked up on enough to insist that I was Rentt Faina. Not that I wanted him to notice everything, but it would have been nice if he figured it out and called me in to talk on his own. He did in fact put it all together, but I still needed to be the one to come to him.

Either way, my plan seemed to be productive. Of course, I couldn't place too much faith in Wolf's personality yet, but I decided I could at least talk to him a bit more.

"That's all the reason you need to believe I'm Rentt Faina? Because our names are similar? That's absurd. I was named after a saint, as so many others are. And Vivie may not be a common surname in this country, but you see it everywhere in the Empire," I insisted.

"Obviously that's not all there is to it. I've got more evidence where that came from. First, it's the way you fight. Second is the place you live. Ultimately you could call it a hunch, but that doesn't matter. Rentt Faina, I don't blame you for the double registration or for hiding your identity, I just want to know why.

"You never had much adventuring talent in the past, and I'm sure you had some vague concerns about your future, but that's not enough reason to give up your identity. You were friendly with the other adventurers in town, and you had strong connections with the info brokers. Even the townspeople loved you enough to toss you fruit and vegetables on sight. I just don't get it. Why wear that creepy robe and mask and go by another name? I was an adventurer myself, so I've met my share of people with strange circumstances. Knew a guy on the run from some nobles, and a guy with such grave secrets that he refused to show his face. I thought you might be in the same boat, but I get the sense you're not, so now I can't help but wonder. Tell me, if you don't mind. In exchange, I'll give you some special treatment. Not a bad deal, am I right?"

By the end, it sounded like Wolf was begging. I didn't know how sincere he was, but he did seem desperate to know. Maybe it was just part of his plan, but I wanted to believe him. Besides, Wolf had more or less hit the mark. I'd cleared up suspicions about me, but Nive was still on my tail, and I did have a secret to hide with regards to my vampirism. However, I didn't know how much I should say or if he would even believe it. As far as I knew, the second I said I was a vampire, he might slay me. Wolf was retired, but he had been a powerful adventurer in his day. I didn't know what rank he had reached by the end, but his intimidating aura was enough to know that while he couldn't go adventuring anymore, he was still far more powerful than me.

To say I was a monster would be suicide, but after our discussion so far, I was feeling inclined to tell him everything. Wolf was a likable man. He had grasped everything about my circumstances except what I needed to hide the most, namely my vampirism, and he offered a deal that would be easy to accept. That was nothing less than kindness, atypical of a guildmaster. Others were busy with collusion and illegal activity. That generosity made me believe he was a good man in earnest. It made me say what I said next.

"Can you prove you're worth trusting? Double registration is against the rules as it is. You're the guildmaster, should you really allow it?" I asked.

Wolf laughed. "Starting with your second question, I think you know double registration's nothing serious. The worst punishment I could give would be to ban you from taking requests for a few days, or maybe charge you a fine, but that's it. Nothing to worry about there. As for the first question, I can't tell you to trust me, but what if we signed a magic contract that says I won't share anything you tell me. Though that might cause some issues, we can work out the finer details. In any case, it'll keep your secrets from getting out. If you still won't believe me after that, well…"

"Then what?" I asked. I wasn't going to be the one to suggest a magic contract. It was true they couldn't be broken, so trust would no longer be an issue, but contracts could have loopholes. While I appreciated his show of trust, I wasn't sure what to say.

"I'll tell you my secret right now," Wolf said. "I used to get laughed at a lot. Back when I was still an adventurer, I had a dream. Everyone thought it was a joke, but it was serious for me. No matter who belittled me, no matter who insulted me, I was set on making it happen. I ended up here instead, but I never regretted being a dreamer. It turns out, Rentt, that I wanted to be a Mithril-class adventurer. That's why I like you. We're a lot alike."

Maybe that wouldn't have meant much to anyone else. After all, reaching Mithril-class was an absurd goal nobody took seriously. It was the kind of bravado you heard from newbies. But the look in Wolf's eyes told me he meant it. We held the same objective and begrudged our own powerlessness, and in that way we had a connection. I had to believe him now. This was everything to me, the dream I brought with me throughout life. Maybe I was being naive or impulsive, but that didn't stop me.

"All right, I trust you, Guildmaster Wolf," I said with a nod.

While I did want to talk, I knew better than to tell him everything without proof. That could wait until after we signed the contract. As long as we had that, I could avoid the worst-case scenario.

We discussed the conditions of the contract in detail before we signed our names. Though I had already as good as confessed, I was going to write my name as Rentt Faina, so I couldn't go first and give it away. Wolf recognized this before I said anything. He took out a quill and then wrote his own name. For as brutish as this man was, he had neat handwriting. I watched Wolf write until he finished and looked up at me.

"All the paperwork forced me to get good at handwriting. If it looks too rough, the staff at the capital all laugh at my proposals. You have to show them that you got an education," he said.

In other words, it was one of the struggles he had to endure as a guildmaster. He spoke to me like an adventurer, but he likely approached nobles with the proper etiquette. His handwriting was so elegant that I would have believed he was a noble if I hadn't seen his hulking arms or the scar on his eye. His was the unmistakable face of an adventurer.

"Here, sign," Wolf said and handed me the paper and quill. I had no more reason to hesitate, so I wrote my name.

Wolf looked at it. "So you really are Rentt Faina," he muttered. I thought he was already certain, but even 90% certainty isn't absolute confirmation. He must have had more hope in me than I thought. He looked like a man reunited with a party member who had stayed behind to hold back a powerful foe.

He was happy I survived. I couldn't see him as a bad person, but maybe I was naive. Maybe that naivety didn't matter.

When I finished signing, the contract glowed and surrounded us in light. The magic had activated. The contract stipulated that nothing I said today could be repeated by Wolf in a way that would harm me. There were more specific terms, but it would take ages to list them all. It was about the same as what I had signed with Sheila. In fact, the terms she had suggested were so perfect I went ahead and copied them. That probably wasn't an issue.

Wolf got straight to the point. "So, Rentt, why register twice when you knew it'd be trouble? Not like you died, is it? You could've kept on adventuring as you had been."

It was hard to believe he didn't already know more, given how he'd said exactly what had happened. He likely didn't know, but to specifically say I hadn't died was comical. I wanted to point out that I had in fact died, but it was too soon for that. I had no idea when the right time to broach that topic would be, but I needed to approach it step by step. I decided to start by describing what happened.

"There were a lot of reasons, but—"

Wolf interrupted. "Might be late to mention this, but you can just talk to me like any old adventurer. No point being polite here. Now if we saw each other at a noble's party down the line, I'd expect some formality, but you can keep it out of the guild," he said.

I immediately relaxed. I'd had to be polite with so many people as of late I had begun to watch my words around superiors as a matter of course. He was right, though; it didn't fit an adventurer.

"Honestly, it's not a big deal anymore, but something did happen to me," I continued.

"What was the problem?"

"I couldn't show my face around people."

"I see, that explains the mask. More than a few adventurers have big injuries though, and the face is no exception. Don't see why that means you had to change your name."

He was correct, and I didn't know how to explain it without revealing too much. The simple answer was I had become undead, but revealing that so soon seemed like a bad idea. I had no way to prove it anyway. Not even Nive could determine that I was a vampire.

As I thought about what to do, I spotted a dagger on the wall. I pointed to it. "Can you give me that for a second?" I asked.

Wolf hesitated for a moment. I assumed he was afraid I might attack, but there would be no sense in that now. If I wanted to kill him, I would have already tried. Besides, Wolf may have had only one eye, but he was likely a mighty warrior. He was confident he could stop me if I pulled anything.

"All right, fine. But what for?" he asked.

I didn't answer him. I just picked up the dagger and rolled up my sleeve.

"Hey now, what are you doing?!"

Wolf panicked and stood up, but it was too late. I had already sliced down the middle of my left arm. It left a long gash, and blood oozed out.

"What in the hell?" Wolf said as he looked at my arm, but his eye soon widened in shock. He witnessed the impossible. "The wound closed up? How? I didn't see you use any medicine or magic." Using either divinity, magic, or ointments would have had the same effect. Wolf knew from experience that this was something else.

"This is why I had to hide my identity. Staying the person I was would have led to chaos down the line," I said.

"Now what's that mean?" Wolf asked.

"I'm undead. This body is no longer that of a human but that of a vampire."

Or so I assumed. I had started to question that as of late, but it was a good enough explanation for the time being.

Of course, my claims startled Wolf. He thought I was out of my mind at first. It was a hard truth to swallow, but I had displayed abnormal regenerative abilities. The only explanation was that I was telling the truth, as he was quick to realize. Still, he had a load of questions.

Wolf finally broke out of his dumbfounded stupor and moved his mouth through force of will. "Wasn't expecting to hear that. Not sure what to ask first, but putting aside whether this is true, how'd it happen in the first place?" he asked.

Wolf still wasn't convinced I'd turned undead. I would have felt the same way if someone had told me that, no matter how honest they were on average. He wanted to know how it had happened, or maybe more so how I had gained the power to quickly recover from wounds. It seemed I would have to start at the beginning.

I told him about everything in order, with the exception of the secret passage in the Water Moon Dungeon. I left that out because of my promise with that mystery woman. That shouldn't have mattered anyway. The important information was that I'd gotten eaten. That part had surprised the woman so much she hadn't included it among the things I couldn't mention. I was only supposed to keep the room a secret, so I was free to discuss transformation.

"This was a while ago now, but I was exploring the Water Moon Dungeon as usual, hunting slimes and goblins."

"The job everyone does when they start out. I hunted there plenty myself back in the day. The Water Moon Dungeon's an ideal hunting ground for solo adventurers," Wolf replied, reminiscing on his early days. He had been a solo adventurer too.

What was nice about the Water Moon Dungeon was how seldom the monsters appeared in groups. Maalt had more solo adventurers than other cities thanks to that dungeon. Having a place to train on your own was a great blessing for those who preferred adventuring alone. If they had a party, then the New Moon Dungeon was much more efficient.

"I searched the dungeon for a while until I found all the materials I needed, and then I headed toward the exit to leave and go home. I was fairly cautious, of course, but when I entered a large room, there was a foe I could never have imagined."

The truth was I had entered uncharted territory, but nothing I said was a lie. It was a large room, after all.

"What was it? The Water Moon Dungeon doesn't have any especially tough monsters. Could've been a unique type or some other abnormality, though, maybe orcs or ogres."

"I wish. I couldn't have beaten those at the time, but I could have run away at least. Not against this, though."

Wolf urged me to continue. "Hm, so what was it, then?"

"It was a dragon, Wolf."

Wolf thought over what I had said. In the end, he scratched his head. "I'd say I don't buy it, but you've got no reason to lie. You must believe it, if nothing else. Problem is nobody else will," he said, implying I might have been seeing things.

Dragons were hard to find whether you wanted to or not. Wolf thought I had mistaken something else for a dragon, a possibility that was far more likely, admittedly. But dragons of this sort did have to exist somewhere. Enough humans throughout history had encountered them and told artists what they looked like, and their depictions of the creatures were clear and distinct. I had seen such artwork in books at Lorraine's house many times, and one of them looked identical to the monster that had eaten me.

What convinced me the most, though, that it was a dragon was its overwhelming strength and unique properties. No human could stand up to that monstrosity. The instant I saw it, I knew that to be true. I had encountered lesser dragons a few times before, such as earth dragons, but that was nothing compared to the powerlessness I felt against the one in the Water Moon Dungeon. Nothing else made me feel so hopeless.

"I know I'm telling the truth. I worried about it being an illusion, but I've experienced illusions before. I'd know if I were affected by one."

"What do you mean?" Wolf asked.

"There was a medicine woman back in my hometown that taught me things. She was a bit of an oddball, and when I told her I wanted to be an adventurer, she said I should learn about poisons and illusions. She had me test all kinds of toxins and hallucinogens, and…"

I paused. I didn't want to remember much more than that. Her method taught me how they tasted as well as how they affected the body. If I couldn't distinguish which was which, she made me do it again. She incorporated these lessons into every aspect of my life, and I never wanted to go through that again. But thanks to that, I could tell whether I was under the effects of an illusion.

I also knew poisons well enough to distinguish right away the type and the cure. I knew I didn't have to worry about poison anymore, so those lessons didn't do me much good now, but I didn't know if I could still hallucinate. I'd already confirmed I was immune to basic types of illusion, but there were still plenty of special ones.

"You've always lived a rough life, eh?" Wolf said and furrowed his brow. He gave me a sympathetic look.

I'd agree it was rough, but I was the one who had gone along with the old lady's suggestion. Her lessons ended up coming in handy, so I couldn't complain.

"Anyway, you insist it wasn't an illusion. I got it. And you're positive this was a dragon. Still don't see how that had this effect on your body, though. Just how'd that happen?" Wolf asked.

My story wasn't over yet.

"Here comes the problem." I hesitated for a moment. I had already decided to tell Wolf everything, but I feared no reasonable person would believe it. It was too late to change my mind, though.

"I'd think the dragon was enough of a problem. There's more?" Wolf asked.

I knew how he felt, but these next details were about how I ended up with this body, the most important part of the story.

"Well, there's no use beating around the bush," I said. "Simply put, that dragon ate me."

Wolf responded right away. "What in the hell are you talking about? If you got eaten, you wouldn't be here right now."

"Normally, yes. But for some reason, after the dragon ate me, I woke up as a skeleton."

"Now hold on a second! I can't process all this! I need some water!"

I wanted to reveal the rest of what happened all at once, but I didn't get the chance. Wolf grabbed a pitcher on the edge of his desk, poured a glass of water, drank it all in one gulp, and took a deep breath.

"All right, that calmed me down. So, you turned into a skeleton? Well, I was an adventurer myself, and I know a thing or two about monsters, but I've never heard of a living human becoming a skeleton. You're friends with that Lorraine lady, yeah? You're living with her now? Heard about anything like this from her?"

Wolf seemed to know about Lorraine too. She was a scholar as her main profession, but she was also an adventurer with Maalt's guild. The guild sometimes asked her to investigate and report on monsters, so Wolf must have been making use of her knowledge.

"I asked her about it but couldn't really follow what she said," I answered. "I know humans can become monsters if a vampire makes them into a servant, for example, but I don't know how you become a skeleton. The bones of the dead can be used to produce a skeleton, everyone knows that, but this is something else. I was most definitely a skeleton at the time, but I was still self-aware. I still remembered that dragon eating me. You don't see skeletons like that lying around any old place, do you?"

Wolf had far more adventuring experience than me, so maybe he knew of exceptions. I asked in the hope that that was true, but he shook his head.

"Not that I've ever seen. The smartest skeletons I've encountered could say a couple words at the most. You look human now, though. Well, you said you were a vampire, but you don't look like any vampire I've seen." Wolf sounded confused, but he got to the heart of everything I said thanks to his experience.

"I look this way because I'm not a skeleton anymore," I explained. "You know about the Existential Evolution that monsters go through, right?"

"Yeah, like slimes becoming poison slimes, or goblins becoming grand goblins. Every adventurer knows about that. Well, besides the ones who don't. The newbies these days don't study enough, especially the ones in the capital. You've got all these folks who get into the job without much thought. The grand guildmaster complains about it all the time."

For my part, I was able to read the books about monsters at Lorraine's house. I loved to read, and there was no shortage of information for me to absorb. For a new adventurer though, without access to a similar environment, they would have to attend classes at the guild or learn the basics from older adventurers. But more and more people wanted to skip those steps. It wasn't so bad in Maalt, but it had become a severe problem in other cities, from what I heard. Maybe the capital was even worse than that. I wanted to go and see it for myself one day.

I nodded. "Yes, there's that. I'm sure you've picked up on this, but when I became a skeleton, I thought maybe Existential Evolution was possible for me too. I was still human on the inside, but my body was pure monster, so maybe I could do some monster things."

"This all sounds nuts, but sure, skeletons can presumably evolve into a lot of monsters that look human. Is that the idea?" Wolf asked, making the most of his intuition.

"Right, I was hoping I could become a ghoul. Then maybe if I kept evolving past that, I could become a vampire or something else that looked human."

"And that's what brought you where you are now? But I was thinking, vampires don't normally go out during the day. Also, do you drink blood or what? Vampires have to drink blood from a couple people each month to survive. Wait, don't tell me our new adventurers have been going missing because of you!" Wolf had become increasingly more serious as we went on.

I panicked and shouted, "No, I didn't lay a finger on them!"

"Probably not, no," Wolf stated right away. "You're not one who'd choose to live if you had to sacrifice someone else. If it came to that, I bet you'd rather wither and die."

His opinion of me was so high it was uncomfortable. But given what the alternative could have been, I was thankful.

"But that leaves the question of how you're getting blood," Wolf noted.

"Lorraine shares hers with me. She knows all about this," I said, deciding to be honest.

I didn't know how much to say about my relationship with Lorraine, but Wolf already knew I lived with her, and he had always known we were friends. While I could claim she didn't notice anything out of the ordinary, I doubted Wolf would buy it. As expected, though, Wolf didn't blame us for keeping it a secret from the guild. In fact, he seemed empathetic.

"Based on what you've said so far, that doesn't come as much of a surprise, but you sure she'll be all right? Vampires suck more blood than a single person can offer, from what I know," Wolf said with concern.

"That's a problem, yeah, but I don't need that much blood. A few drops a day has been enough to quench my thirst. I can eat like a normal person too. After some stuff I went through, however, I started to wonder if I was a vampire at all."

"What do you mean by that?"

"You know Nive Maris, right? She decided I wasn't a vampire."

Wolf held his head in his arms and then downed another glass of water.

After a long period of silence, Wolf asked, "So what's that make you, then?"

He thought about what he'd learned, and that was the question he came up with. Indeed, it was the most important question of all, but I didn't know the answer.

"Who knows?" I offered.

"Hey!"

Wolf shouted and eyed me like I was messing with him, but I wasn't. It was all I could say. Perhaps I could have said it in a less joking manner, but it was too late for that. Either way, I couldn't tell him what I didn't know.

"I wish I knew what I was too, but Nive Maris says I'm not a vampire. Obviously that's going to lead to questions. Before she said so, I just assumed I was a vampire," I said with the utmost sincerity.

I looked exactly like a human, but I had odd regenerative powers. I fed on blood, went out at night, and had evolved from an undead creature. It was natural to guess I was a vampire until Nive shattered that assumption. Maybe I was a new type of vampire not even Nive knew about. If so, there would be no way to know for sure. I was something like a vampire, but that was the most I could say.

"Nive Maris, eh? Right, she's a vampire hunter. You'd figure she knows a vampire when she sees one, but how'd you end up meeting her?"

"I went to the Stheno Company to sell materials, and she was there with a saint from the Church of Lobelia. For some reason, she suspected me of being a vampire."

"You're lucky to still be alive. When she sets her sights on a vampire, she's been known to chase them to the edge of the world. I heard she came to town, but I just thought she was after some vampire. It was you she was after?"

Nive's reputation was even well known among guildmasters, apparently.

"No," I said and shook my head. "She had chased a vampire here, but it wasn't me. My activity around town made her suspicious enough to go after me, though."

Nive acted like a brat, but she was many times more fearsome than she seemed, so it was out of my control.

"That'd mean there's another vampire in this town. As the guildmaster, that'll be a headache for me. Though if Nive Maris is here, maybe she'll hunt it down quickly. Hard to say," Wolf said, bothered by the information I had provided.

Vampires had fearsome strength, but what made them even more dangerous was their ability to hide among humans. Only those with special skills could see the difference between a human and a vampire, so the guild would have to invest all its energy in hunting it down, on top of calling on talented vampire hunters from other regions. I didn't have a great impression of her, but Nive was a famous vampire hunter, and she was already in town. That was good news for the guild...except she didn't think much of the damage she caused around her as long as it helped her hunt vampires.

That would be reason for Wolf to be anxious, but he set it aside. "So how'd you get Nive Maris to leave you alone? Couldn't have been that easy."

"I didn't do much of anything. She used a divinity-based skill called Holy Fire to determine what I was, and I failed to avoid it. I thought I was doomed, but it ended up proving me innocent. I was confused since I thought I was a vampire, but it worked out, I guess."

"Then, that proved you're not a vampire, like you've been saying."

"Supposedly, but what do you think, Guildmaster Wolf? I still need blood to live, so wouldn't I have to be a vampire?"

I asked in the hope that he had some other explanation, but Wolf didn't have an answer.

"I wouldn't know about that," he said with a shake of his head. "But there are too many problems here for me to not take action. A dragon in Water Moon Dungeon? Nive Maris and a vampire in Maalt? And you're connected to all of this? You've got some awful luck."

I couldn't deny that. If nothing else, it was too great a trial for someone who had until recently been a human adventurer unable to climb past Bronze-class. But these events were outside my control. I had to live with it.

"I'd agree I'm a bit unlucky. That's why I feel like more chaos will happen if I stay in Maalt, specifically when it comes to Nive. I think I should leave town for a while," I said, offering my thoughts on the situation.

I could see how these incidents might have revolved around me. However, from a somewhat different perspective, you could also say they revolved around Maalt. I was only getting wrapped up in them, or so I hoped. A change of location at least seemed like a good choice as long as Nive was staying in Maalt for a while.

"Where do you plan on going?" Wolf asked.

"A village called Hathara," I answered.

Wolf knew enough about the surrounding area, and about my history, that he needed no more explanation. "Oh yeah, your hometown. Not a lot of folks from these backwater towns even try to become adventurers, so good on you for that."

I knew what he meant. The town was so isolated that it received next to no outside information. When monsters attacked, the villagers took up weapons and defeated them on their own. They couldn't fight off powerful monsters, of course, so they used incense to ward those off. In a sense, they were an independent village.

Most of the villages around Maalt sought help from the guild when monsters showed up. Now that I thought about it, maybe my village was a bit strange.

"Well, whatever your hometown is, maybe it's best to get out of Maalt for a while. You're right that something could happen again. I thought you might retire from being an adventurer, but if you did, then nothing interesting would happen anymore," Wolf said and grinned at me. "Glad to have a man like you around. Just try not to die. If you aren't already dead. How's that work?"

"I'm not entirely sure, but when I was a skeleton, I had nothing but bones. I don't even know if I have a heart at all." At least, I didn't have a pulse, but I did feel something flowing through where my heart would be. Vampires were killed by driving a holy stake through their heart, so maybe that had something to do with it. Or maybe that had nothing to do with me.

"Man, I don't know what you are, but you sure aren't human. You're right that you seem like some kind of monster, so it must've really taken some balls to come here. How were you planning to justify your double registration to me anyway? Judging by how you reacted, you didn't think I knew so much about your situation, did you?"

He was right about that. I thought maybe he knew something, but I didn't expect he was watching me so closely. Even so, I was positive Wolf would do something about my double registration, thanks to a bundle of papers I brought with me. I set them on Wolf's desk. He gave them a curious look and began to read, but he stopped partway and sighed.

"Nice job compiling all of this. I see why you were so confident, but why give it to me after I already said I'd do what you want? You could've gone without mentioning it and then kept it to use some other time," Wolf pointed out.

The papers listed wrongdoings committed by Maalt's guild. It had details on other double registrations, secret missions, and more. I had received the information from a number of sources, mostly by sending Edel to search for it or by using info brokers. As a final resort, I had even considered asking Laura. She seemed to know quite a bit and might have been open to sharing important information. But she was a client, one to whom I was indebted, so I couldn't bring myself to make that request. Besides, I had other methods.

Edel proved capable, to say the least. He could hide anywhere and understood human speech, abilities that made him excel at gathering information. The results stood for themselves. Of course, Edel's discoveries alone wouldn't be enough to extort Wolf, so I had used info brokers to obtain evidence too. I happened to know a lot of people in this town. The info brokers could be hard to even find, but I knew how to make them gather and sell information. The culmination of my efforts was a set of documents that were almost wasted on fixing my double registration, but that was what I needed them for. Now that Wolf trusted me, I no longer needed them, which was for the best.

"Now, I'd rather not have our relationship built on threats," I said. "Well, this still comes off as something of a threat, so maybe I shouldn't be talking." Now that I thought about it, this actually didn't seem like a great idea. Maybe I shouldn't have brought it up at all. I would've used the documents if I had to, though.

"I don't know if you're a genius or a klutz," Wolf remarked. "Well, whatever. At least you came in here with a plan. If you thought you could solve everything with an up-front approach, you'd be more useless than I expected. In that sense, this proves you caught my eye for a reason." He forgave me right away and then stuck the papers in his desk.

It didn't look like he intended to burn or shred them. I wondered why, gazing at him until he noticed and spoke up again.

"Oh, this? Well, it lists a lot of business even I wasn't aware of. Stuff from before I was the guildmaster. I want to know how you learned all that."

"It's a trade secret."

"Figured as much. I'll have to confirm all this and commit it to memory. Could come in handy down the line."

Wolf wanted to use my research for himself, apparently. I wondered how he'd use it, but I didn't expect him to tell me. Maybe it was time to wrap up this conversation.

"It's yours now, use it however you want," I said. "And as far as the double registration, how are you going to fix it?"

"Hm? Oh, the easiest way would be for you and Lorraine to get married. Then we can consider your old registration a mistake on our part."

"Hey," I complained. I wouldn't mind that much, but Lorraine wouldn't be open to a sudden marriage, so I had to reject the idea.

"I'm screwing with you, there are other ways. We can just erase the name you're not using and say that person doesn't exist, or we can say one of those last names was your middle name and merge the two together," Wolf suggested.

Both options sounded irresponsible, but double registration was evidently not that serious of a crime. Obviously this wasn't the right thing to do, but guilds were such lenient organizations that this was to be expected in some places. If I were to try either of the solutions Wolf suggested, though, I was afraid Nive would come to my doorstep.

"Is there another way?" I asked.

"Man, you're trying to solve a double registration issue. You can't be that picky," Wolf said and furrowed his brow. He still thought about it, though. After a quiet groan, he seemed to hit upon something. "Right, we do have this one system in place."

"What is it?"

"This rule was only meant to be for guild staff, but while double registrations aren't normally allowed, we can use them officially," Wolf explained.

I had never heard that before, but if the guildmaster said so, it must have been true.

If I could have my double registration approved, that would be awfully convenient for me. My two separate identities could come in handy in a few places. Around Nive, for example, I acted as Rentt Vivie, a character with mysterious origins. That's part of why she suspected me, but if she knew I was Rentt Faina and looked into my past, she might have reason to believe I had become a vampire in a dungeon.

In the event she searched the Water Moon Dungeon and found that secret passage, it could be a serious problem. That woman I met at the time was short-tempered enough that if she found out I exposed her, she might be angry. But I could worry about that when it actually happened. I couldn't control what Nive did.

"From what it sounds like, this system would help me out, but can you really do that for me?" I asked Wolf.

He nodded. "Of course. But it's not without its issues. Not sure if you want to accept that or not."

The way he said that sounded suspicious, but I didn't see any other option. This was the best method, so I was willing to accept any conditions.

"What kind of issues?"

"Nothing too complicated. Like I said, only guild staff are supposed to know about this."

That could only mean one thing. "So I have to join the guild staff if I want to use this, is that what you're saying?"

"Well, to put it bluntly, yeah. Can't make you do anything, though. You're trying to reach Mithril-class. If you can pull it off, then I'm sure you'd rather focus on that. You've got enough problems with your body the way it is, so you wouldn't want to take on even more work," Wolf answered.

He sounded generous, but I wouldn't know if he truly was until he said more.

"Thing is, if you don't use this system, then your only options for dealing with double registration would have to be what I told you before. Marry Lorraine, erase one of your registrations, or merge them together. Each one sounds like it'll create problems for you. But if you join the guild, there'll be some bonuses in it for you. The rules would permit you to keep your double registration as is, and you'd get access to the guild's information network. Also, the point of this system is to let staff members mingle with adventurers and learn what they have to say. You can keep adventuring as you have been, rising through the ranks. There even used to be a Mithril-class adventurer who was a guild staff member. Also, you can use the guild's facilities in every city for a reduced price, if not for free, you can get bargains from participating stores, and you can make a little extra on the materials you sell. Nothing but advantages, really," Wolf said, concluding his list of amazing benefits.

He came across like an overzealous salesman, but it did sound appealing. I could continue to live life as I had been, but now I could use the guild's offerings as much as I wanted, buy goods for less, and sell materials for more. I was ready to demand I be hired at that very instant, but I knew better than that. Everything Wolf mentioned was a plus, but there had to be minuses. I could think of one.

"I'd have to do work for the guild, right? How much time do you think I have?"

I had a surprising amount, actually. Enough I could train a disciple and study magic on a whim, but I didn't need to mention that. I wasn't going to take more work if I didn't have to.

"Fair enough," Wolf said after a bit of thought. "I'll give you as little work as possible. We can just put your name in our registry, how's that sound? Might have to ask you for something on occasion, but we can talk it out when that happens. Always possible I'll give you orders during an emergency, but if you have such a problem with that, then just tell me and we can give you a pass."

Again, it was all convenient. It didn't seem to be a joke, either, from the way he looked at me.

"I appreciate it, but why go that far?"

"Like I said, I expect a lot from you. That hasn't changed. Maybe you're a monster now, sure, but this conversation told me that you're still the same on the inside. No issues here."

Was that sincere? I supposed it was, judging by the look on his face. That was the expression of an adventurer with conviction. The trouble now was I had no excuse to say no. I could object for the sake of objecting, but this was such a strong offer that it would be unfair of me to do so. Maybe that was the idea, but there was nothing else I could do now.

"Fine, hire me as a member of the guild staff. I'm my own first priority, though, as long as you're all right with that."

"No problem. All right, now that that's settled, there's something else I want to know," Wolf said and looked up at me.

"What?"

"You wore that mask because you couldn't show your face, but that was because you were a skeleton or a ghoul before, right?"

"Right. Nobody wants to see dry, rotten, fully exposed muscle," I said.

Wolf imagined it and grimaced. "Makes sense. But now you may or may not be a vampire, and look more or less like one, don't you?"

"True." I nodded, knowing where he was going with this. "You're wondering about my mask?"

"Yeah, are you wearing it because you can't show your face when you're acting as Rentt Vivie? I'm curious."

I shook my head. Not that it wasn't true, but my biggest reason was more simple than that. "Actually, I just can't take it off."

"It's cursed?"

"You got it."

Wolf jumped to his feet. "Mind if I try pulling it off you?" he asked.

I didn't feel like I could refuse, so I nodded. Wolf grabbed the mask from both ends and tugged with all his might. I almost fell over, but the mask didn't budge.

"Come on, Rentt, you can plant your feet on the ground better than that," Wolf complained, but I was trying hard enough as it was. My inhuman strength was still no match for him. He said he couldn't go adventuring anymore, but it seemed to me that he could have continued the job just fine.

Wolf tried to remove the mask a few more times but to no avail, no matter how much he pulled and shook it. The mask couldn't be taken off by ordinary means, as Wolf finally came to realize. I told him I got the mask at a vendor, but he looked confused.

"Cursed goods shouldn't have been able to enter town in the first place. That's interesting, I ought to look into it," he said.

After that, I left Wolf's office. "Rentt Vivie" was to be treated as a staff member for the guild, and I would receive my staff license later. A lot happened, but overall, negotiations went well.

Before I left the guild, I asked Sheila if she wanted to have dinner with me. The food itself wasn't the point so much as I wanted to tell someone who knew my situation about what had transpired today. I hadn't planned on telling Wolf everything, but I couldn't change the fact that I had. At least I had a guild staff member on my side in the form of Sheila. She could deliver messages between Wolf and me. Also, while I wasn't asked to do much work, I was still supposed to be working for the guild now.

That made Sheila my senior at the workplace, so I wanted to ask her about the rules. I knew something about their regulations and their expectations from adventurers thanks to the pamphlets they kept by the reception desk, but I knew nothing about the internal rules for staff members Wolf had mentioned. I assumed they had something like those pamphlets for staff members as well and I'd be told to read them later, but I wanted to know the basics before that.

Sheila got the sense I needed to invite her for these reasons, so she agreed to come to Lorraine's house after work.

The food was always good. Tons of dishes were arranged on the table, every one of which was a collaborative effort between Lorraine and Sheila. Some blood was mixed in, but it tasted a bit different from normal. This was more delicious than usual, but I wondered why.

"Did you season the food differently today?" I asked. Lorraine cooked on her own most of the time, so maybe Sheila's involvement changed the food somewhat, but that didn't seem to be all. I didn't know how to explain it, though.

"Well, today's cooking contains both my and Sheila's blood," Lorraine explained. "I said she didn't have to go that far, but she insisted."

That did explain the complex flavor. I didn't know if it was because their blood tasted good combined or because both their blood was good on its own. It was nice of Sheila to offer her blood, though.

"Sheila, you didn't mind?" I asked her.

"I did to some extent, but you're a vampire and you need blood to live. I've known that ever since we made our contract, but you've been getting all your blood from Lorraine. She says it's only about a bottle a month, but I'm afraid that's going to make her sick one day, so I thought it might be a good idea to try mine," she said. Wolf worried about the same thing. The last bottle of blood Lorraine had given me was almost empty too, so more contributors were appreciated.

The food with blood was, of course, meant only for me. Lorraine and Sheila had regular meals.

"In that case, I'm happy to have it. But on to the matter at hand," I said and changed the topic to what Guildmaster Wolf had told me. Mainly, I informed them that I revealed my situation, that he was understanding about it, and that my double registration could be solved if I joined the guild staff.

"I see," Lorraine responded. "Sounds like there isn't much of a problem, then. All those documents you collected weren't good for anything in the end, apparently." Lorraine had helped edit the files I assembled. Her input made it easier to understand the content of the documents, in fact. But it ended up being a waste of time.

"I just gave them to him. Sorry I made you help out for nothing," I said, apologizing.

Lorraine shook her head. "If he trusted you, then threats wouldn't have been the best idea. I would've recommended keeping them a secret in case something happens down the line, but you were never one to be proactive about these things. It's fine," she said.

She didn't say I couldn't keep them a secret, however, because she knew I could. I just didn't want to.

"Still, a loophole that lets you keep your double registration? I vaguely remember that rule existing, but I'm surprised the guildmaster was so quick to bring it up. It hasn't been used in Maalt in decades, as far as I know," Sheila mentioned.

"Really?" I cocked my head. I figured the rule wasn't told to adventurers but was in common use by staff.

"Yes, it's for staff to use when they want to survey or gather information from adventurers. We don't need to work as adventurers to get that information nowadays, though, so nobody does it. There isn't much point," Sheila explained.

It sounded like this system was as good as dead, and yet Wolf had thought about it immediately.

"I'm guessing the guildmaster was thinking about swaying you with that from the start," Lorraine said.

"Probably, but why go that far?" I pondered.

"He's been interested in you for a long time. I imagine he's been considering how to make you join the guild for just as long. That'd include looking into ways he could hire you while you're still an adventurer. He really thinks a lot of you."

In other words, this was an option he'd had in mind ever since I had become a Bronze-class adventurer. However, I doubted he thought I was that important.

"That does sound like something he would do. He thinks about these things a lot. It's easy to get the wrong idea from how he looks, but I hear he's pretty smart. He's a good person, though," Sheila interjected, providing supporting evidence for Lorraine's speculation.

If that was true, he had me in the palm of his hand. But manipulating someone like me couldn't have been that hard, as I tended to go with the flow. I decided not to worry about it.

This wasn't bad for me in any way, and if something did happen, I could think about it then.

Relaxing too much could lead to pain down the line, though, as I had come to feel as of late.

When dinner was done and everything was explained, we saw Sheila home then relaxed in Lorraine's living room.

"It seems like your double registration problem is solved now, so what name are you going to go by?" Lorraine asked.

"Oh, I'll be fine as Rentt Vivie for a while. Changing my name while Nive is still around could be dangerous," I said.

Lorraine nodded. "Well you have a point there. But I'm surprised that solution existed. I thought they were going to erase one of the names."

"Yeah, he suggested that at first. He also said I could marry you to fix it, but there's no way I could've done that."

Lorraine spat out her wine. "What's that supposed to mean?" she said, scowling.

"I could have married you and taken the name Vivie, then said they forgot to erase my previously registered name. I was shocked when he said it, but in the end, there was no need to resort to that. Anyway, let's sleep for the day. Tomorrow we're buying what we need for the journey, right? Good night."

It was about time to gather everything we needed, so I had plans to go shopping with Lorraine the next day. I could stay up all night if I wanted, but Lorraine was only human.

"Yes, right. Good night, Rentt."

I waved goodbye and went to my room. I hoped to see some neat magic items tomorrow, but we were only going to buy what was necessary, so that probably wasn't happening.

"Marriage, huh?" Lorraine muttered when she was alone. The word sounded odd to her.

She was already well past the average age for marriage, but plenty of women married old acquaintances at her age. If he kept the name Rentt Vivie, it would also mean marrying into her family.

"Marriage, huh?" Lorraine repeated and closed her eyes. She tried to imagine it, but it gave her an itchy sensation.

"Oh! That looks interesting," I said and ran up to a street vendor.

They had a number of mysterious magic items. Most usable magic items were found at magic item-exclusive stores, where they were appraised and sold with a written analysis, but they could also be found at vendors.

Appraising magic items was expensive. When adventurers found magic items in dungeons, they usually went to the guild or a magic item shop to get them appraised, but if they were clearly useless, or if they were appraised and turned out to be useless, they turned up here. Common examples of the former were pins that did nothing but bounce in place, singing flowers (whose songs were not good, they just sounded like noise), and torches that flared up and went out at random intervals. Examples of the latter were magic swords that hadn't been enhanced at all or medicine that looked like healing potions but did nothing except cause a stomachache.

Not all the items found in dungeons had applications. Nobody bought them unless they were curious, they knew the hidden uses for these items, or they were children who wanted toys. In the end, they found their way to these vendors.

"Looks like nothing but children's toys and garbage. Why do you want these things?" Lorraine muttered and furrowed her brow.

We were at the market to buy assorted goods. There was preserved food, portable grindstones, clothes, potions, and more. Lorraine could make high-quality potions on her own, so we didn't need to buy those necessarily, but gathering the materials to make them would be a pain, so we were purchasing those. Monsters could also attack us on the way there, so we needed containers for any useful materials they might drop. In the past, I used Maaltan magnolia leaves to wrap up orc meat and bottles to contain slime fluid. When it came to things like that, buying from bigger stores got you better quality than vendors, but the vendors sold for cheap. I went to the big stores when I needed something for a job, but this was a personal journey. Somewhat lower quality wouldn't be an issue. I did have to watch out for goods that couldn't be trusted, however.

"The fact that they seem worthless makes me want them. If you only buy things that are useful, it gets boring."

Lorraine reacted to my argument by holding her head in her hands. "Are you getting philosophical with me? I don't get it."

I would have retorted that it was about adventurous spirit, but I knew who would look like the stupid one in that exchange. I wanted those magic items anyway, I couldn't help it.

"Well, you can use your money however you like. I just bought a book with no practical use, so I do understand where you're coming from to some degree," Lorraine conceded, holding a thick, leather-bound book she had bought from the last vendor we'd visited.

It was called *Monster Cooking: How to Make Low-Quality Parts Taste Good*, a foreboding title. Cooking with monster parts was normal, but the "low-quality" aspect made me wonder what they meant in particular. Maybe slime, but even that could be made into something palatable. I could only pray I never had to use this book.

"Oh, there are some more book vendors," Lorraine pointed out. "Rentt, I'm going to check that out. Go ahead and look at magic items all you want. Let's meet by the bench on the east side of the central square in about an hour."

She wandered off to an area packed with book vendors, presumably to buy more weird books. I had no idea what good they would be, but we were alike in that way. That's what had kept us together for the last decade.

That left me to look at magic items, so I reached out toward a mysterious board that hovered about three centimeters off the ground.

"Oh, I'm sorry."

The person next to me apologized. She tried to grab it at the same time and bumped my hand. It didn't hurt me at all, so I didn't mind, but I thought it bizarre that anyone was interested in this item. Myself aside, of course. But I hid how I felt and looked up to talk to her.

"That's okay, I'm—" I began, but then time stopped.

"Is something the matter? Is there something on my face?" she asked.

The answer was that there were eyes, a nose, and a mouth, but that wasn't what left me speechless. I had seen this woman before. She had blonde hair and blue eyes. Her face made her look young, but with the promise of growing into a beauty in a few years.

Her appearance clashed with the leather armor and sword she wore. I never expected to see her here.

"No, nothing. Do you recognize me?" I asked.

"Wait, have we met? A mask that covers half your face, a black robe…" She trailed off as she racked her brains.

It seemed like she forgot, but then I remembered something. My mask looked different from the last time we had met.

"Sorry, how's this?" I said and changed my mask into a skull shape that covered my whole face. I also put on the hood of my robe and lumbered around suspiciously. She opened her eyes wide.

"Oh, are you Rentt?!" she screamed. I changed my mask back and took off my hood, nodding.

"Yes, that's right. Long time no see, Rina."

"Where have you been?! I've been looking for you all this time. I was so worried," Rina said with as much concern as she claimed.

"I'm staying at a friend's place," I admitted. "I've been doing adventurer work as usual, but mostly at times when nobody else is around. That's probably why we haven't run into each other."

"That explains it. I go out early in the morning most of the time. But I'm glad you're okay."

Rina was still a novice, after all. Jobs for beginners were posted at the start of the day and were highly competitive, so new adventurers had to get up early. Of course, there were simple extermination requests for slimes, goblins, and other basic monsters that were available at all times, so you could get by without waking up early if you were so inclined, but monster slaying was a challenge of its own. There were safer jobs than that if you went to the guild early, and they paid better for the amount of work too. For example, there were requests to pick herbs or to carry luggage for more advanced adventurers. Some of these jobs were surprisingly risky, however, so it was best to take a close look before accepting them. But novices didn't know that.

As for Rina, apparently she had managed to survive since we last parted ways. We were only together for a short time, but I taught her a lot of what I knew, such as the best places to hunt, the best stores, what precautions to take as an adventurer, and other general knowledge lessons. Maybe that had helped her.

"Well, I'm doing all right. As you can see, I shouldn't have the problems I did before anymore. Anyway, how have you been? Are your adventures going well?" I asked.

"Yes, of course. When I put your teachings into practice, everything went better than ever. Actually, I just joined a party the other day! With a boy and girl around my age, though."

I had spent my ten years of adventuring alone, so the idea of a party stung to me, but Rina's communication skills were far greater than mine. I was jealous. Well, not really. I had been invited to join parties myself. At least once, I swear. I just liked going solo.

But it was good to hear that her party members were one man and one woman. That shouldn't have been too dangerous for her. If they were around the same age too, it didn't sound like they were approaching Rina with any ill intent. A lot of adventurers in their mid-twenties took advantage of people that way. Meaning those around my age, but I would never do that. In any case, I tried to probe her about this party to see what they were like.

"That's nice. Are they good people? How'd you end up in a party with them?"

Rina promptly answered all my questions. "They're great. The boy is a swordsman named Raiz. He's a little reckless, but fights his hardest. The girl's name is Lola. She's a mage who can use healing spells. I joined their party after we got in contact with each other through the guild and talked for a bit."

There were a lot of reasons not to trust guilds, but Maalt's guild had Wolf in charge, so it did its job better than most. They paid special attention to the safety of their adventurers, so their death rate was low. The guild also put effort into training new adventurers, and when anyone came to them about forming a party, they performed an examination to ensure they didn't get stuck in a party with suspicious characters. Many new adventurers had mana, spirit, or other special abilities that made them common targets to kidnap and enslave. But thanks to the measures this guild went through, anyone introduced through them could be trusted to an extent. On top of that, the names Rina mentioned sounded familiar.

"Are you talking about Raiz Dunner and Lola Satii?" I asked. They had taken the Bronze-class ascension exam with me. Rina's description fit them perfectly, so they came to mind right away.

"Yes, that's right," Rina confirmed, nodding. "You know them?"

"Yeah, back when I took the Bronze-class exam, they entered the dungeon with me," I said.

"They told me about a nice man named Rentt Vivie. Was that you?!" she exclaimed.

They'd already told her what happened, it seemed. If they knew me best for being nice, though, that was disappointing. I'd rather have been known for something cooler, though something too cool could be hard to live up to. Maybe if it was something like "Rentt, the Man Eaten by a Dragon," or "Rentt the Bone Man." Or not. Coming up with cool titles wasn't my strong suit.

"I don't know how nice I was, but that was me, yes."

"But I thought your last name was Faina," she whispered. Nobody was there to listen to us, except maybe the owner of that stall. She must have been wary of that.

"Well, some things happened with that," I said just as quietly. "Just remember I'm calling myself Rentt Vivie for the moment."

"Okay, but isn't it strange how you've met both me and my party members before? And we happened to run into each other today, too. Maybe there's something to this," Rina said with glee.

Coincidences could bring about unexpected encounters. Like when I ran into the dragon, or when I met Nive. I hated coincidences. This chance encounter with Rina was the only one I had enjoyed anytime recently. She was like Lady Luck, in a sense. Maybe this meant my visit to Hathara would go well too.

"That reminds me, there's another strange connection between us," I said.

"What?"

"When I went to the blacksmith the other day, I ran into a man named Idoles Rouge. He said he was looking for a woman named Rina Rouge. Would that happen to be you?"

He claimed to be in search of his younger sister, an adventurer, but her name was different from the Rina I knew. I had assumed he was seeking someone else, but I didn't know of any other adventurers named Rina who had come to town lately, and I knew a lot of what transpired in Maalt. There was a high chance he meant this Rina, and as expected, the name I mentioned made her eyes open wide with shock.

"That's my brother, yes. I didn't know he came to look for me."

"I knew it. Well, don't worry, I didn't tell him about you. He was the very picture of a knight, but he didn't seem fit for finding someone in a small town like this."

From what I remembered, he came across like a big-city dweller, refined in his behavior and with a nice, sincere personality. He seemed like a man who took his work seriously, but that made him stand out in a chaotic town like Maalt. I still spotted him walking around on occasion thanks to how poorly he blended in. He drew the eyes of a lot of women, too. Knights were always popular with the ladies. Not that I was jealous or anything.

But anyway, if he was walking around so much and still hadn't found Rina, he couldn't have been that good at gathering information. Maalt might not have been that large, but it was still a proper city. There were so many people that searching around at random was akin to looking for gold dust in a desert.

Knights weren't familiar with the information sources outside the big city, so they had to resort to asking around at pubs. Rina didn't seem like she frequented those places, and none of the tough guys who did were likely to know her. Her name wouldn't ring any bells either. But if he went around to shops like when I met him at the blacksmith, they wouldn't share information on their customers with him. Shopkeepers were especially wary of knights from the big city, so they shared as little as possible and tried to get them to leave sooner than later. Idoles had a lot of hurdles to overcome.

If you're wondering how I knew all this, it was thanks to Edel's information network. Edel had gained control of about half of the puchi suri in Maalt, so I had ears all over the city. If I wanted to investigate anything, I only had to tell Edel and I'd have an answer within an hour. They couldn't get near the Latuule house, however. A lot of mysteries surrounded that house. The Latuule family had numerous magic items, so those must have kept them out. Tiny monsters couldn't have been that hard to repel. Either way, Edel's network was more than a little useful.

"My brother is the prime example of a knight," Rina said with a little smile. "But that doesn't mean he's inflexible. Back when I lived at home, he took me to all kinds of places."

That was something of a surprise. From what she told me, Rina came from a family of nobles. Most knights came from that background. That meant Rina was a wealthy heiress, so I questioned why she was adventuring in a small town to begin with. But putting that aside, bringing a rich heiress with you to any old place was a strange thing to do.

"Was he a good brother?"

"Yes, I'd say so. I wouldn't be the same without him."

"Did you become an adventurer because of him?"

"Yes, I did at his suggestion. I basically ran away from home to become an adventurer. He taught me some swordsmanship, so I did okay, but I'm not great at the social aspect of the job. I used to work in the capital, but that didn't work out, so I came here."

The adventurers in the capital were much more vicious than those in Maalt. It was a dog-eat-dog world, as I understood it. That was a bad environment for a newcomer. The guild in the capital sometimes recommended working in other cities first, sending new adventurers to Maalt on occasion. Maalt was easy on newbies thanks in large part to the guildmaster. I heard he was friends with the grand guildmaster in the capital as well.

"In that case, should I have told him about you? I acted like I didn't know anything, but I felt kind of bad about it," I said.

"Probably," Rina replied. "My parents are one thing, but I don't think my brother would be here just to drag me back home. Maybe I should look for him."

"Then what'd be a good time for you? I can tell him. You'd rather not go to the trouble of searching, right?"

It wouldn't be much trouble for me, thanks to Edel. I could just pretend I ran into him by coincidence and ask if the Rina he was looking for was the one I knew. That would have to make him happy. Maybe my appearance would make him suspicious, but as long as I didn't ask to meet in any strange places, that wouldn't be a problem. If I suggested we meet up in a decrepit shack outside the city, that might put him on guard, but maybe it'd be worth a try. No, probably not.

"Really?" Rina asked of my offer. "Okay, if it's not too much trouble." Then she told me when she was free.

I promised I would tell him, and after a bit more chatting, we exchanged contact information and parted ways. It was about time to meet up with Lorraine.

"Made some big purchases today," Lorraine said upon returning home and gazing contentedly at the stack of books on the floor.

I had carried the books from the vendor in my magic bag on the way back, but she had demanded they all be taken out as soon as we arrived. She wanted to get straight to reading them. I understood the feeling. When I bought books, I couldn't wait to read them. She was already reading one of them as we walked home, though. I wanted to tell her to stop in case she ran into anyone, but Lorraine had the skill of a Silver-class adventurer. If any passers-by approached, she could avoid them without even seeing them, so I had no real reason to warn her. However, it set a bad example for any children out there. I wanted to tell the orphans that she was a bad lady.

"So, like I said before, I'm going out for a little bit," I told Lorraine.

"Great, be careful out there." She waved her hand with disinterest. The book had her captivated already. She was hopeless, but at least she was listening.

After that, I left the house.

What I had told Lorraine was I met Rina at the market and promised to deliver a message to her brother, so I needed to head out to meet him. I'd previously explained to Lorraine about how I'd met Rina in a dungeon, so she was interested in meeting her, but that could wait for another time. Rina seemed busy with her adventuring work, so I didn't know about inviting her to come mess around.

Edel's subordinates were tracking Idoles. Edel led the way ahead of me, so I followed after him. My mask had covered my whole face last time I'd met him, so I adjusted it into that form again. Any on-lookers would see a suspicious man in a skull mask and robe following a rare black puchi suri. I probably looked like a diseased grim reaper. In fact, I heard the occasional gasp from those who saw Edel and me. At least I looked human, but it was still an ominous sign. Nobody paid attention to me when my hood was off and I reshaped my mask, but seeing me like this during waking hours would be frightening. Oh well, Idoles, wouldn't recognize me any other way.

Eventually I came across a familiar man, rugged and clad in knight armor. I hurried toward him.

"Sir Idoles," I called out to him. He turned around and looked at me, saw my sketchy clothes, and cocked his head.

"Ah, I met you outside the blacksmith the other day," he said.

"Yes, right. You remember me?"

"I could not forget that outfit if I tried. Your voice sounds different, though. It used to be a bit more..."

Idoles didn't finish his sentence, but I suspected he meant to say how hoarse I'd sounded. My vocal chords were barely functional at the time, so my voice was just awful. At least now I could talk like a normal person. But I couldn't tell him I had moved up the undead ranks, so I came up with an excuse.

"My throat was injured, but it's better now. Sorry about that." That was a common enough occurrence. Idoles didn't question it.

"Is that right? I am glad to hear it. You appear to be an adventurer, but I am knight myself, so I understand what manner of damage monsters can do. You are lucky it was not permanent," he said, offering his sympathy.

The highest class of saint could heal injuries that normal recovery spells and divinity could not, but they seldom offered their assistance to any given knight or adventurer. When he counted me as lucky, that's what he meant.

"Yes, I suppose so." I nodded.

He nodded back then seemed to recall something. "Now, what in the world brings you to me? I presume you sought me out for something."

"I did. Last time we met, you mentioned you were looking for your sister. I believe you said her name was Rina Rouge."

"Ah, yes. Did you find her?"

Idoles drew closer to me. It almost looked like he was about to grab me by the collar and shake me, but he kept calm. His face, however, could not have been closer. His handsome mug approached with such force that it made me jump.

"Yes, probably."

"Probably? What does that mean?"

"The Rina I know told me her last name is Rupaage."

"I see, that is a different name. Did you not find her, then? What compelled you to investigate her in the first place?"

Her name was different because she had every intention to hide her identity, so she wouldn't want to reveal that when asked under normal circumstances. The fact I knew who she was must have seemed unnatural. Idoles squinted at me but didn't seem that distrustful. I decided to be honest.

"I didn't investigate anything. She told me when I asked her. I'm an adventurer from this city, and she's the only Rina I know. I mentioned you when I was chatting with her recently, and she said you were her brother."

"Is that right?" Idoles asked, relieved. "My apologies for thinking you suspicious."

"That's fine, everyone worries about their family. Don't feel bad," I said.

"This may be rude, but you are much more amiable than you look," Idoles replied, confused.

Maybe that was true. I didn't think so, but I came to him purely out of goodwill on this occasion, so I knew why it looked that way.

"I'm just normal. So, I have a message for you from Rina." I told him her desired meeting time.

"That would be a bad time. I must soon return to the capital for a while, but perhaps another time. May you deliver a message to Rina for me? I can pay you," he offered.

"I'm happy to do it for free. I owe Rina one anyway," I said. Without her, I wouldn't still be around. I could leave his message on the message board or whatever else he wanted.

"You owe her? Hm, I would like to hear the story behind that, but I can wait to ask her. Please see to it you tell her, then," Idoles instructed. He told me the next time he would be in Maalt and the place he would be waiting and then left.

The appointed time was about a month from now. I didn't think knights got so many breaks, but maybe they had more free time than I expected. I didn't know, but I headed off to the guild to leave the message for Rina. I knew where her inn was, but when we had met at the market, she'd said she would be exploring a dungeon later. This was the surest way for her to receive it.

Chapter 4:   The Journey

"Anything left to do? Have you forgotten anything?"

Lorraine stood at the entrance to her house early in the morning and asked me as if she were my mother. I remembered all the business I had wrapped up over the last few days, including delivering Dragon Blood Blossoms to Laura and relaying Idoles's message to Rina. Everything was taken care of. Probably. The problem when it came to forgetting things was that you forgot them. Maybe there was something I wouldn't remember no matter how hard I tried. That was worrisome, but if I couldn't remember, it must not have been that important.

"Well, I don't think so. If there is, I'll think about it when we get back home," I said, repeating what so many forgetful men had said before.

Lorraine looked fed up. "At least put the slightest effort into remembering. But it's not like we'll be gone forever, I suppose. That's fine, let's get going," she said and opened the door.

It was time to travel to my hometown of Hathara.

Maalt was far from the center of the country, but it was still big enough to be called a city. Nothing compared to the capital, of course, but a fair number of travelers passed through it. Many carriages were halted near the gate to Maalt, their coachmen shouting from their seats. A good amount of people wanted to get on the carriages, paying the coachmen en masse. It was a lively sight.

Most of them were heading to cities in the west. Each section of the station had carriages that went to different cities, so once you got used to the place, it wasn't hard to find what you were looking for. The coachmen yelled only so those who didn't live in Maalt could more easily find them. Lorraine and I had nothing to do with that thriving scene, going instead to an area of almost dead silence.

"Is this it?" Lorraine asked when we stopped at a carriage.

"Yeah," I replied and nodded. "It always makes me anxious, though. I can't believe this thing can make it to Hathara." I had ridden it there plenty of times, but every time I saw it, I worried all over again. Where most carriages were drawn by horse, this one used a giant tortoise. Horses were the stereotypical animal employed by carriages, but other animals could be used as well. It was still mostly horses, but depending on the route and the speed required, there were sometimes better options.

After horse-drawn carriages, the next most common were dragon carriages, which used an animal that was similar in shape to a horse, but was actually related to drakes. They were faster than horses, had more stamina, and didn't fear monsters. However, more than one horse could be used at once, and they were easier to handle thanks to being less powerful. Overall, horses were still more convenient, so these drake creatures were used only when speed was of the utmost importance. They were also too expensive for commoners; they were meant more for nobles and knights.

This carriage, however, used an animal called a giant tortoise. They were stronger than horses, but they were also slower. The trade-off was their extreme durability. They could hide in their shells if any monsters attacked, so they were often used for dangerous or mountainous roads. The route to Hathara wasn't as well maintained as the road to the west, and it was much steeper, so giant tortoises were ideal. Regardless, it was hard to see them as anything but a huge tortoise. You would think it'd take over a century to reach my hometown. In reality, though they were somewhat slower than horses, they walked fast enough. Their legs were longer than that of a normal tortoise, giving them a mildly amusing appearance.

"It always makes it there, right? Then why worry? Now, where's the coachman? Oh, there he is," Lorraine said, spotting an old man.

While all the coachmen in the previous section were shouting, this one was smoking a pipe and reclining against his carriage. He didn't seem enthusiastic at all, but I could understand that. There was little point in shouting out to people heading east. There were only so many, and most of them were also in the transportation business, so it was a waste of energy.

"Old man, we want a ride to Hathara. What do you charge?" Lorraine asked.

The old man looked up. "Five silver coins. You'll get lunch, but if you want more food than that, get it from the towns we stop at on the way. We'll go when more people arrive, so wait around till then," he said.

It was hard to say if five silver coins was cheap or not, but Hathara was just about the final stop. Considering it took about a week to get there and lunch was included, it was likely on the cheaper side. The westbound carriages were even cheaper. More people traveled west, so they had more passengers. Plus, they had a paved road to tread, so it took less time to travel the same distance compared to eastbound carriages. It was inconvenient to live in the middle of nowhere in more ways than one, so I seldom returned home. I had no money, and walking back would be brutal.

"Then one gold coin should cover both of us. Here you are," Lorraine said and paid right away. I took out five silver coins to give to Lorraine, but she stopped me. "Pay me when we get home. I don't need more coins to carry around," she insisted. She acted more manly than I did. Maybe I was just effeminate. I felt bad, but I could just do what she asked and pay her on the way back. That, or I could pay for our meals in town.

The fun of journeys was to eat delicacies you could only get abroad. There was often the typical peasant food, but sometimes you found something special that the locals thought nothing of but turned out to be incredibly rare cuisine. Examples included great winter frog eggs and fried curtis mants, a type of killer mantis. Both were delicious, but they looked terrifying to eat. They would probably be available at the towns along the way, so I could make Lorraine try them.

"Now I guess we wait. I'm looking forward to this," Lorraine said.

"Yeah, me too," I agreed.

What was Lorraine going to say about these delicacies? Maybe it would be cruel to have her eat them. She was from the city, so they could be rough for her. I imagined it as we waited for people to arrive.

"It's time to go. Get on," the coachman said after a number of passengers gathered.

We got in the back and looked at the others around us. Including us, there were six passengers in all. I didn't know if that was a lot or a little. There was a young girl with a middle-aged man, an old married couple, and that was it. The old couple could have been a pair of amazing mages, but I didn't sense the least bit of mana, so they probably weren't. That or they were so monstrously powerful they could hide all their mana, but again, not likely.

Given where we were going, though, the coachman at least must have had some combat talent. Monsters seldom appeared on paths created by humans, but it did happen. Monsters weren't the only danger on the road either. There were thieves too, so we would have to fend them off if it came down to it. We couldn't make old people and young girls fight. Lorraine was young, I supposed, but she was a skilled adventurer and mage. Making her fight was fine.

The coachman sat in his seat with a whip in hand. When he struck the tortoise's shell, it woke up and began to lumber forward. It was painfully slow, but only until it left the city.

"This is my first time on a tortoise carriage. I'm surprised it's so fast," Lorraine said, a bit impressed.

I looked out from beneath the canopy and saw the scenery scrolling by at a considerable pace. It was certainly faster than running by foot. I popped my head out of the driver's side to check out the giant tortoise, and its legs moved at a brisker pace than any tortoise I had ever seen. It was slow to start, but it accelerated to a decent speed. Their horsepower was the reason they were valued. They were also mild-mannered and could take a beating. Still, they could bear to be a little faster.

"This is as far as we go for the day. Sorry you'll have to camp outside, but we're far from any town. There aren't many monsters around, so it should be safe," the coachman said and stopped the carriage.

Of the passengers, only Lorraine looked shocked. "I see, so this is what it's like for rural people," she remarked insultingly.

I admit I was somewhat annoyed by what she said, but, at the same time, I could see where she was coming from. The road to the west had only half a day's travel between each town. This would never happen on the way to a big city, but we were on a road to the countryside, so the first day of travel always ended like this. They could have built more small villages on the way, but the ones that had existed here decades ago had been destroyed by monsters. The monsters in question had been slain at the time, but the survivors hadn't wanted to live in the area anymore, so they had moved either to Maalt or further west. This land had been left uninhabited ever since.

Memories of that disaster had faded over time, so someone could take the initiative to start up a new village, but people like that only appeared so often. It wasn't easy.

"You've done plenty of camping, haven't you?" I asked Lorraine.

"I guess so. You dragged me around and made me learn to camp back in the day, so there's that," she replied.

It almost sounded like she was holding a grudge, but it was a joke, of course. I had actually dragged her around though. Lorraine couldn't do anything back then. Now she was brilliant and adept at everything, but at the time she hadn't even known how to gather wood to start a fire. She knew some spells but had never thought about how to use them in everyday life. That was why she couldn't camp on her own, but now she was handy to have around.

"Mr. Coachman, should we cook dinner?" Lorraine asked.

"We've got some dried meat, but you can do that if you want," he answered.

"Then we will. For three bronze coins, we can make something for you too."

"Hm, then do that, if you don't mind," he said and handed Lorraine the coins. She asked the same of the other passengers and collected their money.

"Let's get cooking, Rentt," she instructed.

Before we had left town, we had bought up a fair amount of food. It was a bit marked up in price, but it was no serious loss for us. I pulled food and a cooking pot out of my magic bag and began to prepare while Lorraine drew a magic circle on the ground. Then she cast a brief spell and conjured fire. The other passengers looked on with fascination.

Mages weren't hard to come by if you looked for them, but they seldom revealed their magic to others. Spells for use in daily life in particular wouldn't usually be used while camping, as it could be a waste of mana. But Lorraine had a lot of mana, and her magic circles were as simplified as possible, so they were efficient enough that they hardly cost energy. At least, I assumed so. I didn't know that much about Lorraine's magic, so there was a lot I couldn't say for certain. Whatever the case, this was easy for her. The magic circle itself used elementary knowledge, but it looked beautifully crafted. If I learned from Lorraine, I could do the same eventually. Presumably.

When I had to camp on my own, I would start a bonfire without a magic circle. Usually I did it by casting a spell on a piece of tinder, but it consumed too much mana to keep the fire going, especially back when I didn't have much mana to begin with. Lorraine's method was more common among adventurers due to the importance of conserving mana.

Anyway, while I was thinking about all this, we finished preparing to cook. I put the ingredients in the pot and told Lorraine to cast a spell. It caused the ground to rise up and take the form of a hearth. I set the pot on top of it, and then Lorraine used magic to fill it with water. I could have done the same, but I feared I might accidentally overflow the pot, so I left it to Lorraine again. She inserted the exact amount of water we needed, checked the contents of the pot, and closed the lid. Once it finished boiling, we would have a hastily produced but fairly tasty stew. You could hardly call this cooking if you got it at a restaurant in town, but while camping, it was a decent feast.

Some time later, we took off the lid and let out the steam, along with a nice aroma. The father and daughter, the old couple, and the coachman all watched with anticipation. We handed out bowls of stew, along with ham and cheese sandwiches on rye bread.

"All right, shall we eat?" Lorraine asked, and we all dug in.

The old couple prayed before they began, but I couldn't hear what they said. It was probably a prayer from some regional religion. When you're away from civilization, you see villages with all sorts of strange gods. I didn't criticize them for it, or think much of it beyond remarking on how deep their faith must have been. I didn't even know what god the shrine in my village was meant for.

The stew was favorably received, so much so that the group was willing to pay for our meals the rest of the way to our destination. That was what we bought all the food for in the first place, so it was fine by us. My magic bag had enough space to fit a giant tarasque, so storing a week's worth of food for six people was simple.

When dinner ended, the time to watch for monsters had come. The area was relatively safe, but it wasn't devoid of threats. Watchmen were necessary. There was only one coachman in this case, so the passengers with the most stamina would have to take turns standing guard. That meant me, Lorraine, and the middle-aged man. Honestly, I was the most fit for the job thanks to my lack of a need for sleep, but I couldn't point out that I was undead, so the coachman and the rest of us switched places periodically. First was the coachman, then the middle-aged man, then Lorraine, and lastly me. I slept just a tiny bit during the coachman's turn and stayed up the rest of the time. Lorraine and I chatted around the campfire until something caught our attention.

"I think we have uninvited guests," Lorraine whispered.

I sensed someone in the woods behind us.

We stared at the forest until we knew what they were.

"They don't seem to be people. More like the remains of people," Lorraine muttered sympathetically.

"A few decades of death doesn't mean much to the undead. Maybe if you're the sort that needs to consume something to live like I do, but not these ones."

"Right."

They were zombies.

Lorraine and I observed the putrid walking corpses. They had tattered clothes, bamboo spears, and hoes. These monsters were called zombies, and they were another type of undead. They differed from me in that I was a vampire and required the energy derived from blood to survive, but zombies had no such limits. Perhaps in exchange, zombies tended to be brittle and weak.

That being said, they were still a great threat to ordinary humans. Scholars believed living creatures avoided placing too much stress on their bodies by structurally preventing themselves from exerting their full strength, but zombies were already dead. Their bodies could move and stretch in otherwise impossible ways. Their heads spun all the way around, and their limbs flailed as if they had no joints. These attributes could even make them a surprising nuisance for adventurers.

However, the biggest reason to avoid them was their stench and their filthy bodies. They often carried diseases. It would be fine if they wandered around at random, but we couldn't let them near the camp. They had to be defeated right away. Lorraine and I were quick to come to the same conclusion. That left the question of how to beat them.

"Will magic work?" I asked Lorraine.

"Well, probably. You'll get contaminated if you fight them, so this looks like a job for me," she said.

Lorraine pulled out her wand and approached the zombies. She waved her wand around as she drew near. I wondered what she was doing, but then I noticed that the wind began to blow from us toward the zombies. She cast a spell with no incantation. It was a low-level spell, but to cast it like it was nothing displayed Lorraine's skill. I could do the same, but only with the couple of life spells I had used repeatedly over the last decade, so that wasn't saying much. Those spells didn't require much restraint. That wasn't the case for the spell Lorraine used, though. It had to be kept stable to continue blowing wind, so it must have been difficult. The point was to keep the stench or any stray chunks of zombie flesh from flying toward us.

When Lorraine arrived in front of the zombies, they began to circle around her. Signs of life had drawn them to our camp, but their eyesight seemed poor. They showed no interest in me or anything else around the carriage and instead focused solely on Lorraine. Because there could be more waiting for an ambush, I remained on guard but noticed nothing around me. Zombies weren't smart enough to sneak up on anyone, either. There was no reason to worry too much. I did sense some more zombies in the distance, but they were steadily decreasing in number for some reason, so they weren't an issue.

Maybe they were killing each other, maybe they were fighting bandits, or maybe they had run into other adventurers. For the time being, I chose to remain cautious, but it was best to turn my attention to Lorraine.

"Yes, this should be good enough," Lorraine said once she was surrounded. "Nobody else is nearby? Good. 'Wind, I command you to blow. Fire, I command you to burn. Become a whirlwind that incinerates my surroundings. Paloom Igni Su Turbo,'" she chanted.

Flames materialized around Lorraine, followed by a gust of wind. The wind swirled around the flames and created a blazing tornado. The zombies' rotten brains seemed to still just barely work because they tried to flee from the whirlwind. But it proved too powerful; the red flames burned them to ash.

Casting fire magic near a forest seemed suicidal, but only for an amateur mage. One of Lorraine's caliber could control their magic well enough to prevent the fire from spreading. If I tried it, though, we would have a wildfire on our hands. The thought was so frightening I couldn't work up the will to try.

After a little while, all the zombies had been incinerated. The spell had fearsome power, but Lorraine was still holding back. Her incantation could have been better, and she even included a line to suppress the strength of the magic. When the blazing tornado shrunk and disappeared, Lorraine stood unharmed where it had once been. She turned toward me.

"Rentt, come over here," she said.

I wondered what she wanted and walked over, finding a pile of ash and magic crystals. They had clearly come from the zombies, but I would have thought that they'd have been blasted away. The level of control she had over her spells was a thing to behold, but now I saw why Lorraine called me here.

"I thought burning them to ash would be enough, but after gathering these all together, I guess not. I could use holy water, but conveniently, I have you here. Can you take care of this?" she requested.

In other words, the ash and the crystals were full of evil energy and miasma. I was supposed to use my power to purge it.

Many impure monsters required purification upon defeat, which adventurers handled in a number of ways. The method Lorraine mentioned was to use holy water on the corpses. It worked well enough on all but the most powerful monsters, so this was a relatively common tactic. But most adventurers didn't bother to do anything. Holy water cost money, and few adventurers carried it around at all times. If they took a request to vanquish impure monsters, any adventurer with common sense would bring some along, but many chose not to because it was too much effort or it would cut into their profits.

Instead, they left the remains alone. This was a bad move because the corpses of impure monsters would curse the land they died on, eventually making it uninhabitable, like with the Tarasque Swamp. The miasma from zombies was only strong enough to make the land around their corpses infertile for a few years, but it was still best to do something about them. That was why Lorraine gathered up all the ash in one place. She probably collected the crystals just so we could sell them later, but they required purification as well.

When monsters were burned to ash, like in this case, purification was sometimes unnecessary. If they had been scattered by the tornado, the evil energy and miasma would be dispersed enough to make it harmless. It might make passers-by a little sick or slow the growth of plants, but nothing more than that. That still wasn't good, but it was acceptable.

But Lorraine was a sensible adventurer, so she kept holy water on her and would have used it if I wasn't around. I was, though, so she didn't need to. Holy water was expensive, so it was best to conserve when possible. In contrast, any divinity I used would eventually recover. It showed how useful divinity users could be.

"I guess I'll do that, then," I said. I held my hands out to the pile of ashes and crystals and began to fill it with divinity. Both purification and healing were something I had an instinctive sense of how to do, which was a nice aspect of divinity. The proper way to do it was probably more efficient, but to learn that, I would have to join some religious organization somewhere. That, or I would have to ask a freelance divinity user. There weren't many of them, but they did exist.

I slowly poured more divinity into the pile until the wicked aura from the ashes and crystals dissolved into the air. It seemed to be purged, so I let out a sigh of relief. I knew how to do it, but I'd never properly learned, so I was unsure if my method was correct. It didn't seem to cause any problems this time, at least, but there was one curiosity.

"The walking fertilizer strikes again. This is what happens when you purify something?" Lorraine murmured as she stared at the purged ashes.

"Stop calling me that," I demanded. "Judging by these results, though, I have to admit it's not inaccurate," I reasoned and gazed at the ashes as well. There were sprouts growing from them, and I knew they had grown thanks to my divinity. Plants couldn't grow on corrupted land, so this proved the purification had worked, but this entry on the list of reasons to call me walking fertilizer left me astounded.

"Oh well, it's not like this does any harm." Lorraine concluded. "It's safe to pick up the magic crystals now, I take it?"

I looked at the crystals and confirmed there was no miasma or evil energy left. "Yeah. I wouldn't expect much money for zombie crystals, though."

"Probably not, but I can use them to research necromancy. They'll be perfect for that."

Lorraine said it like it was nothing, but necromancy was a forbidden art of sorts. It wasn't banned by the government, and you wouldn't be executed for using it, but it was considered immoral. Necromancy itself was said to be a legendary technique that had been lost to time. All that remained was some ominous hearsay. That was probably the reason for Lorraine's research, but she could very well bring back necromancy if she tried, and that was kind of a scary thought. But I didn't expect Lorraine to be interested in that.

"Why research necromancy?" I questioned.

"It could help to understand the undead. Necromancy has long been forgotten, so researching the undead who continue to exist might be faster, but this could help somehow," she answered.

Now I understood. "So you're doing it for me?" I asked.

Lorraine looked at me like I was stupid for asking. "Obviously, yes. I'd rather not dabble in the forbidden arts otherwise. Well, it's not like I'll be executed for researching it, so it's not as if it'll be a serious issue," she replied.

It felt like I was putting a weight on her shoulders. "Sorry," I apologized.

"That's not the right word for the situation, Rentt. There's something else you could say."

"Right. Thanks for all your help."

"Please, we're friends. Don't worry about it."

Some time passed after that.

"Oh? Someone else is here. Do we have actual humans this time?" Lorraine said.

I noticed it too. The zombies I had sensed in the distance were gone, so this must have been what had fought against them. Whatever it was that approached us, there was only one. There had been a considerable number of zombies out there, so if this was a human, they were strong enough to take them all down by themselves.

This was someone with a great deal of skill. It would be fine if they were an adventurer, but if they happened to be a thief or something, it could get ugly. Lorraine and I stood on guard and prepared for what was coming.

"A kid?" Lorraine whispered when something appeared from the forest.

She couldn't have been right. "Why would some ordinary kid be in the middle of nowhere?" I argued. Maybe it wasn't completely impossible, but it was highly unlikely. It did look like a child, though, except for certain traits that stood out.

"Methought the zombies fled this way. Mayhap you fellows smote them?" the child said in an incredibly archaic manner. It was a style of speech nobody had used since before my grandparents' generation. We still understood what she meant, though, so we could at least communicate. There were old folks in my village who spoke like this, and Lorraine came from a world dominated by the elderly.

"Yes, it was me who took them down. You can see their ashes right there," Lorraine replied to the supposed child, pointing to the pile of ash.

The child nodded. "Ash? A mage, are you? I see, you do have incredible mana. Those zombies would be but a trifle to you. Yet 'twas my failure to slay them all that let them get here. Forgive me," she said modestly.

That meant these monsters were her target for some reason. "What were these zombies?" I asked out of curiosity.

"Ah, there was a village hereabouts four decades ago, where once there were villagers. Zombies need no sustenance and hence will remain until they are vanquished. Howbeit, not a soul has tread this land since, and the zombies have thus been in a dormant state all this time."

While zombies didn't require any food, that made them sluggish and inactive. If nobody was around to attack, they ceased to function at all. That was called a dormant state. Something must have awakened them, presumably this child when she had entered the ruins of the village.

I didn't know what to say about that. That was what it meant to be undead, I supposed. Undying was not the same as living. You continued to exist, but if there was nobody around to remember you, then you might as well have been dead. I thought it was beyond tragic, and my feelings must have crept into the look on my face because the child got the wrong idea.

"Worry not, I buried them all so they shan't return. 'Twould be pitiful to leave them as they were," she said as she approached the ashes. "I happen to be a master of the divine arts, and purging evil is my specialty. Shall I also purify these ashes? Wait, hm?"

From what she said, I thought this could lead to some trouble, but it was already too late. If she could actually use divinity, then there was no hiding it. And I knew she spoke the truth because I could see that her hands were full of divinity. That explained how she could so easily hunt zombies.

"The evil energy has already been purged? Burning them to ash wouldn't have this effect. Did you use holy water, perchance?" she asked.

Lorraine took out a bottle of holy water. "Yes, I carry some around for times like these."

The child was convinced. "Hohoh, you are wise compared to the average adventurer nowadays. The undead lurk all about, and they must be cleared away after their defeat to avoid disaster. Long ago, we all kept holy water on hand, but now— Ah, excuse my grousing."

"Whatever," I replied vaguely, thinking about how she was speaking to an undead at that very moment. I wasn't trying to hide it, but I wasn't keen on telling a divinity user either, so I waited to see what happened.

"'Twas all purged without a trace, though. Holy water wouldn't be so thorough. Wait! Grass? In the ash? And 'tis giving off divinity, no less! Are you hiding something from me?!" she frantically asked.

We had kept our distance out of caution, but she moved right next to us in an instant. It was no joke, and I didn't need divinity to see she had remarkable skill. However, if she tried to attack, we did have some room to counterattack, so we were still fine. Either way, I sensed no hostility and saw no reason to draw my weapon.

At any rate, Lorraine responded to the child. "We're not trying to, but we've hardly had a chance to talk yet. We don't even know each other's names," she said with the utmost honesty.

We were hiding that I used divinity to purge it, technically, but nothing she told her was a lie.

The child seemed to agree with her. "Forsooth, I have yet to introduce myself. Is that why you're so on guard?"

The child acted innocent, but it was all a sham judging by the deft way she had approached us a moment ago. She seemed to think on her feet too.

"Hrm, I have not seen adventurers with such backbone in some time. Tell me your names. Of course, I will start. I am Alhildis, a meager adventurer. I'm Gold-class! Behold," the child said and presented her adventurer's license.

When adventurers encountered each other, this was the easiest way to establish trust. Her shining gold license appeared to be the real deal.

We were still wary, but Alhildis kindly tossed us her license. "Check it until you're satisfied," she said.

There was no reason to assume it was a fake now, but some thieves did copy adventurer's licenses to disguise themselves. After all that had happened with her so far, that seemed implausible in this case, but I looked the license over just to be safe.

Both Lorraine and I felt we'd suspected Alhildis too much when we otherwise wouldn't have if not for her appearance. We analyzed the license until we determined it was legitimate and then threw it back to her.

"Sorry we doubted you," Lorraine said. "But you have to understand how we feel. We never see elves around these parts."

Yes, elves like Alhildis were extremely rare in this region. She had beautiful pointed ears and sky blue eyes. Her golden hair was cut in a medium-length bob. She had the stature of a girl around ten years old but came across like an old woman. It was impossible to not be suspicious.

"Yea, of course. I, too, was wary because I sensed powerful magick. You're not alone," Alhildis said with a smile. She felt so innocent and lackadaisical that this admission came as a bit of a surprise. But only a bit of one, given that elves were known for being crafty.

Despite looking like a ten-year-old human, she could have mentally been decades, even centuries old. At that age, she was a creature beyond our comprehension. But in all honesty, so was

I from their perspective. Lorraine, Alhildis, and I were all different beings from each other. That was kind of interesting, but I couldn't bring myself to mention it.

"That's good to hear," Lorraine said. "Oh, I should introduce myself too. I'm Lorraine Vivie, a scholar, adventurer, and mage. And this is—"

"Rentt," I interrupted. "I'm also an adventurer. My main weapon is a sword."

Talking about your fighting style was a standard part of introductions between adventurers. We knew how Alhildis presented herself when she showed us her license. It said she was a mage, but based on her use of divinity, that seemed to be a front. These descriptions didn't mean much, and it wasn't like Lorraine and I used magic or swords exclusively either.

We showed her our licenses too, though they didn't tell her a lot. They were good for proving your identity, but little more than that.

"Hm, Lorraine and Rentt? I'll try to remember. As for myself, mayhap Alhildis is too long a name. I ask you call me Hilde or Hildi," Alhildis said.

Lorraine and I looked at each other. "Hilde, then. Should we treat you as an elder, or...?" Lorraine trailed off.

Hilde was an elf and likely far older than us. From what she said about adventurers back in the day, this was obvious. Nobody had walked around with holy water since at least my grandparents' generation. If she was our senior, it was hard to know exactly how to speak to her.

"Talk to me as you have been," Hilde said. "I'm treated as a beldam all too often. As you can see, I look young for my age."

She looked more than a little young. I had no idea how old elves were supposed to look at any given age, though, so I looked to Lorraine to see if she knew. Her eyes told me it was beyond her. But Hilde said she was young, so we could go with that, I decided.

Lorraine nodded and chose not to ask about her age any further. "Then how about we just treat each other like adventurers? So, Hilde, why are you here?" she asked.

Depending on Hilde's answer, we could end up in a fight, but after the cordial conversation, I hoped it wouldn't come to that. Besides which, while she seemed to be messing around, she had to be powerful. These kinds of people were always insanely strong when it came to adventurers. She was Gold-class, meaning she rivaled Nive, if not surpassed her. Elves also lived long enough lives to learn a plethora of skills, and they had spirit magic particular to their race. I didn't want to get on her bad side. Lorraine asked about her objective in the hope of ensuring we were safe, and I felt the same way. I didn't know if Hilde guessed our intentions or not, but she replied in a sincere tone.

"Oh, right. 'Tis a long story, but in short, I am an adventurer who hails from the capital. I took a job to restore the village of Toraka by smiting the undead who dwell here. The deed was done just moments ago when I defeated their boss, but the zombies were so great in number that a few managed to flee this way. I do apologize," she said.

Toraka was the name of the village that had been destroyed in this region many years back. I had heard about it from the adults in my hometown. Lorraine seemed to infer the same from our conversation. Hilde mentioned it fell to ruin four decades ago, a number specific enough to assume she spoke the truth. There was nothing else around, so I couldn't imagine any other reason she would be here.

"No need to apologize, we beat them already. Well, Lorraine did, not so much me," I said.

"I don't mind either," Lorraine added. "They weren't a big deal."

They probably would have been a bigger deal to everyone sleeping in the carriage. However, even if Lorraine and I hadn't been there, the coachman could have dealt with them well enough. Maybe he would have been injured, and he couldn't have purified the corpses, but those were the risks you had to take while on the road.

"But were there monsters aside from these ordinary zombies? You said something about a boss," Lorraine asked.

"Oh, there was," Hilde answered. "A zombie soldier, but merely a single one. 'Twas a hunter from the village, methinks. The undead retain the abilities they had in life, you see. 'Twas good with a bow, but no serious threat. That is all I have to share. What about you?"

"We're not on a job or anything," I said. "Just on the way to my hometown."

"I see, so that carriage is headed to some village. Seeing as you're a man and a woman, are you married? Courting?" Hilde asked intently.

"No," I promptly stated. "It's complicated."

"I told you I'm a scholar, right?" Lorraine continued. "His village sounds interesting, so I thought I'd come along." She spoke the truth but subtly dodged the question.

Hilde, however, seemed to be understanding. "Forsooth, these untouched lands have ancient ruins and folktales that could prove interesting. Hm, now I know your objectives. Onto my main question, then."

Lorraine and I had hoped we could deceive her in the end, but from the sound of it, we had failed.

"How did you purify these ashes? And what are these plants? Tell me, if you would be so kind."

All I could think about was how much I didn't want to tell her. The more secret weapons I had in store, the easier life would be down the line. But it wasn't as though I ever did much to hide my divinity. I hadn't thought it was anything special back in the day. But now I could do much more, and nobody knew it aside from those I told about my circumstances. I thought about what to do until Hilde said something that put an end to that.

"Howbeit, I already know the answer. Rentt, you're a divinity user, aren't you?"

This surprised me a little. Only a little, because Hilde said she was a master of the divine arts. She probably had techniques I didn't know myself.

Hilde elaborated. "Normally I wouldn't know, but for some time after one uses divinity, one can see some residue left in their body. It requires a close look, so apologies for invading your privacy."

We didn't know if that was true or not. I'd borrowed one of Laura's books on divine arts but hadn't read enough to learn anything. Maybe it would have helped if I had read more. However, it was a surprisingly difficult read. I could imagine what magic was supposed to look like well enough to learn spells from books, but written descriptions of divine arts were often hard to grasp. At least I could get a feel for some aspects of divinity already. The biggest problem was how much of it seemed to be theoretical. Someone would have to teach me the basics before I could handle divine arts, and that sounded like it would take a long time. Without that knowledge, I had no way to tell whether Hilde was lying. Lorraine couldn't use divinity at all, so she would have no way of seeing it. That meant we had to guess if Hilde spoke the truth from her tone and attitude.

That turned out to be impossible. Lorraine and I looked at each other then gave up. Nothing in Hilde's expression gave us a hint. Maybe this was typical of elves who lived for so long, or maybe this was a skill particular to Hilde. Either way, we were at a disadvantage. Even if Hilde were bluffing, I knew she was almost certain she was right. Holy water couldn't purify as thoroughly as divinity. I hadn't realized until I had become keenly able to sense it, but the stronger your divinity became, the more sensitive you were to evil energy and miasma. When you looked at it through that lens, holy water's purification powers were inferior to divinity, or at least different in nature. Holy water was more suited to precision, and more was required to cover a wider area. Maybe you could just put it in a spray bottle, but that would probably be blasphemous. Would holy water spray bottles sell? Not right away, I'm sure, but they would certainly be useful. First, they would need to be advertised.

Anyway, now I had to consider what to do about Hilde. After she'd deduced as much as she had, it was likely best to tell the truth. Her suspicious staring had gotten painful, and unlike my being a vampire, this wasn't the kind of information that would get me killed. She might try to make me join some religion, which would be annoying, but it couldn't be anything worse than that.

"Yes, you're right, I purified the ashes. I can use just a tiny bit of divinity, but I don't know how to use divine arts or any other proper techniques with it. I don't really believe in any gods either, so I can't just go join any religion," I admitted. If I could use those techniques, maybe I could have hidden my divinity, frustratingly enough.

"I knew it," Hilde said. "Your lack of faith may be a problem." She furrowed her brow.

"What do you mean?" I asked.

"As I said, your divinity is something any reasonably talented user can see. Divinity users are rare, as you no doubt know. Every religion would like more. Nobody proselytizes better than saints, so religions have fought over divinity users since time immemorial."

Despite that, I had yet to be scouted by any religion. Not when I met Nive and Myullias, nor when I met Lillian. Maybe they were being considerate. Lillian could simply not have known I had divinity. As for Nive and Myullias, Nive might have been too zealous to say anything about it. If she had tried to make me join her religion after all that happened, I would have said no anyway.

"Can't I just tell them I'm not interested?"

"Yea. Howbeit, to do that every single time would get tiresome. There are also some who use rough methods. You had best learn to hide your divinity," she said.

Good advice, but I didn't know where I would start. I had read a book on divine arts and still barely understood it. The language was too unique for me to pick up anything without a lot of work.

Hilde seemed to notice my hesitation. "I can teach you, if you wish. I belong to no religious organization," she offered.

That sounded true enough. Elves had their own faith, and few believed in religions started by humans. For elves, their faith was also more a part of their life. The Holy Tree was the subject of their worship. Well, not all of them, and they didn't deny the existence of gods. It was complicated.

At any rate, Hilde's offer sounded good to me, but I had other business to attend to. Besides, would she teach me for free? Probably not, and I was afraid to know what she'd demand.

"You want something in exchange, right?" I asked honestly.

"Nay, I can't make you do anything," Hilde said with a smile. "May I have that grass over there, though?"

I didn't expect that. She referred to the grass in the ashes. There were many little sprouts. I was going to leave them and continue my journey, so it was no skin off my back.

"Why?" I asked, still curious about her reasons. The grass gave off some mild divinity, but I didn't see much use for it.

"I don't know how much to tell you, Rentt, but I presume you were blessed by a plant spirit. Therefore, plants grow from that which you purify. There were once many like you, but no longer. The number of plants that produce divinity has drastically decreased. These are rare, so I want them. Well?"

That left me with a lot to think about. If this was all she wanted, I had little reason to refuse. Hilde might tell more people I was a divinity user, but it was too late to prevent that. She didn't need the proof, though. Certain people would just know.

"All right, take it. In return, teach me all about divinity."

Still, we had plans. There was no time to learn right away, and Hilde couldn't have had time to teach when she was in the middle of a job.

"I'll teach you in full soon enough, but I can drill the basics of hiding divinity into you for now. Don't worry, 'twill not take long. You're on night watch duty? I can teach you before you're done," Hilde said.

She sounded like a swindler I saw in town who peddled a method of losing ten kilograms in a single week. I could imagine the title of her book, *Divinity For Dummies: Learning the Basics in a Single Night, Hilde-Style*. It sounded sketchy to me.

Hilde noticed me narrow my eyes. "I happen to be adept with the divine arts. I won't show you the depths of divinity, but the surface can be scratched in but a night. Magic is similar, I believe," Hilde argued and turned to Lorraine.

Lorraine seemed to know what she meant. "Well, you could learn to control mana and use life magic in that time," Lorraine said based on her experience with Alize. Certainly there were some people who could pick that up in one night. Some couldn't, but it was a matter of talent.

"In any case, try it. 'Twill only take till dawn. A hasty lesson to be sure, but once you get a feel for it, you can improve on your own," Hilde said in a way I could understand.

The divine arts were nothing like magic, so I didn't know how it should feel to use them. Maybe I couldn't learn in a night, but Hilde would be in the capital. Even in the worst-case scenario, I could go visit her to finish the lesson, so I decided to take her offer.

"'Tis done. Your divinity is hidden well enough that I don't notice it. The average divinity user won't stand a chance of finding out," Hilde said, her back to the orange sky.

I had spent the night learning the basics of the divine arts and putting them into practice until I had mastered something that at least seemed right. I could control and hide my divinity, but I wondered if these were actually the fundamentals because it wasn't easy. I needed this to avoid problems down the line, though, so I couldn't complain.

"I have to keep this up all the time?" I muttered.

"'Tis easy once you get used to it. Think of it as nonstop training till then. 'Twill feel as natural as breathing in a week at the earliest. Look," Hilde said and unleashed her divinity.

She'd been hiding her divinity the whole time, so I didn't know exactly how much she had until then. Now that I saw her release it, it was dozens of times greater than mine, if not hundreds. Maybe even more than that. Nive was similar, but this destroyed any confidence I had grown since then. If she could hide all this divinity, then her claims of being a powerful divinity user were true. I had only just started to dabble in the divine arts, though, so it was hard to say for sure.

"You have so much more than I do that I don't know if I can follow your example." I gave my honest impressions.

Hilde shook her head. "If I lost out to a young buck who didn't know the first thing about the divine arts, what good would I be? Now, this will do for the basics. Henceforth, read that book you showed me and keep up your studies. The book's lessons are accurate, and you should have a feel for the divine arts now."

I hadn't known if the contents of Laura's book were correct or worth following, so I'd asked Hilde about it. She'd given it her seal of approval and said it was fine.

"All right, but what if there's something else I don't understand?"

"Then ask me. I work from the capital, so come visit if you have questions. Here is my contact information and my registration number with the guild," Hilde said and handed me a piece of scratch paper. "Now, 'tis time I take my leave. The other passengers of your carriage may be startled if they see me. Tell Lorraine I said goodbye. I'd like to discuss academics with her sometime. Farewell."

She grabbed up the grass in the ashes and hurried away. Her gait was firm and confident.

I almost wanted to call out to her to come back. We'd only just met, but she was oddly affable.

"Is she gone?" Lorraine asked, noticing me and rubbing her eyes. She had been asleep.

I didn't need to sleep at all to stay healthy, but Lorraine was only human. She could likely have gotten through night watch duty and just been somewhat sleepy, but the road ahead was going to get even rockier, so she wouldn't be able to sleep in the carriage. Monsters were most likely to appear from here on as well. If she fought while tired, then she might hit me on accident, and that wasn't preferable. Lorraine recognized as much, so while she did want to talk to Hilde, she made sleep her priority.

Lorraine and Hilde had a surprising amount to discuss. Hilde had lived for so long that her knowledge and experience were even of value to Lorraine. Reading books was fun, but there was plenty they couldn't teach you. Lorraine was an avid reader, and even she was keenly aware of that. It made sense that she would want to hear what Hilde had to say.

"Yeah, she told me to tell you she says goodbye. Also, she says to come to the capital if you need to know something about divine arts."

"The capital? I don't go there much."

"Me neither," I said.

In my case, I simply wouldn't get much adventurer work in the capital, but Lorraine avoided the place because she found it bothersome. When she wanted something that was only available in the big city, she sent a letter to an acquaintance in the Lelmudan Empire. Even the biggest cities in a small country like Yaaran were like Maalt to Lorraine. But while she didn't go frequently, she had been a few times, unlike a full-fledged country boy like myself.

"Well, there's no time at the moment, but I'll think about it. Much as I'd rather not go to the capital, it's not impossible I'll be convinced."

"All right. Should we wake everyone up now? It's time for us to depart," I suggested.

We went around waking up the passengers and the coachman. We had to leave as soon as the sun began to rise if we wanted to get anywhere. Ideally, we wouldn't have to camp two nights in a row.

None of the other passengers seemed to know what had happened. Both the zombies and our (well, really just Lorraine's) removal of them and Hilde's visit to our camp all night were entirely unknown to them. The zombies were already dead, so there were no signs of life from them, and Hilde was an experienced enough adventurer that she knew how to conceal her presence from the average citizen. From the perspective of the passengers, we had a peaceful night of camping. Well, the coachman did seem to notice something, but anyone who would drive a carriage through these unpaved roads had to be strong in their own right. If he noticed, then that would stand to reason.

The carriage raced under the morning sun and reached a town just before sunset. Nothing happened this time, much to my and Lorraine's relief. I wasn't here as a bodyguard, so I preferred to avoid the anxiety of that line of work as much as possible. Not that the thieves who appeared on these country roads would be much trouble to take down. The monsters who showed up on the road weren't a huge threat either, but it was more work than I wanted to attend to.

"Nice, looks like I'll get to sleep in a bed tonight," Lorraine said as she exited the carriage.

We had been sitting for so long that our bodies were stiff. We stretched as we walked, producing popping sounds.

The path here was severely bumpy. The road to the west was well maintained and free of rocks that would impede a carriage, so it was a smoother ride. I wished they would take care of this road too, but considering the time and money it would take, I didn't expect that to ever happen. I'd fund it myself if I had the money, but I didn't. I just had to give up on it.

"I'm looking forward to the food more," I said. The cuisine in most towns was normal, but this village had the delicacies I previously mentioned. I couldn't wait to see how Lorraine reacted to that, but then she said something unexpected.

"Oh right, this village is famous for its solest and gettamba. I can't wait to try them either."

I thought these mystery words sounded like the names of magic spells.

Lorraine furrowed her brow. "What? You've stopped in this town a few times before, right? The winter frog egg dish is called solest, and the fried baby curtis mants are called gettamba."

Now that she mentioned it, I had heard those names before. The names weren't as impactful as the dishes themselves, so they didn't stick in my mind. You could see the tadpoles in the winter frog eggs, and the fried curtis mants were still identifiable as mantises after being cooked, with five or six of them brought out on a plate. Any woman who would eat them had to either be from this town or have a lot of guts. Most would be too taken aback to even put them in their mouths. But Lorraine was different, it seemed.

"You're interested in trying those? That's, well, I don't know what to say," I said, at a loss for words.

Lorraine guessed what I was getting at. "Do you think that's bizarre? Well, you're not wrong, but they were listed in a book

I bought from a street vendor the other day. When I saw they were available nearby, I wanted to give them a try," she said, reminding me that she'd bought a book about cooking monsters.

I thought Lorraine bought every book regardless of genre to sate her thirst for knowledge, but I didn't expect her to be sincerely interested in the subject matter. Maybe that desire for knowledge made her open to just about everything, though, knowing how Lorraine was. She seldom let biases get in the way of anything, for better or worse. That was why she'd still accepted me when I had become undead. She really didn't have to show the same generosity to food, though. I didn't even know if I would be all right with those dishes; it had been so long since I ate them. At least the flavor was fine. Well, it would have to wait until dinner.

With that, we headed to the inn. The coachman had made arrangements for us to stay there in advance, so our late arrival wasn't a problem. Any time we arrived would have been fine though, knowing how far from civilization this town was.

The steaming bowl contained jiggling eggs covered in a gelatinous substance. They were transparent enough to see the gigantic tadpoles inside. That was solest. Next to it was a big plate of not just five or six but twenty or thirty fried mantises in a large pile. That was quite the sight to see. In fact, I wasn't hungry anymore just looking at it. I didn't want to touch the gettamba.

Seated next to me, Lorraine loaded her plate and ate them like any other food. "What, Rentt, are you not eating? Well, maybe it won't taste good for you without any blood," she said, considerate enough to whisper the last part.

That wasn't the problem. I simply didn't like how the food looked. Hathara never had cuisine so flagrantly uncivilized. We barely had winter frogs or curtis mants around Hathara, though, so that was probably part of it. They ate these monsters around these parts partially to cut down on their numbers while they were still small, but there was no need for that when they weren't present to begin with.

"No, that's not it. I'll eat some, I swear," I insisted, crying internally as I put a paltry amount of frog eggs on my plate. They were firm, and I could see that the giant tadpoles were still moving around inside. Remorseful about taking their lives, I put them in my mouth and touched the gelatinous substance with my tongue. It had a strange texture, soft but soaked in juices from the stew that gave them a fine flavor. I worked up the will to eat more, biting into a tadpole. A gentle taste filled my mouth, contrary to their sickening appearance. It was mildly sweet, while the juices were savory. I could never get enough of these, if only they looked like anything normal.

Next was the fried curtis mants. Surprisingly, there were only so many of those left too. I was at the same table as Lorraine and the other passengers, all of whom ate without a fuss. I heard all the crunching sounds and knew they came from the mantises, so it should have been obvious. I reached out to grab a curtis mant and made eye contact with it. Disturbed and unable to tolerate staring at this bug in silence any longer, I shoved it in my mouth headfirst and chomped it in half. The crisp sensation spread throughout, along with a refreshing taste atypical of fried food. I thought it was good, perfect to go along with some beer, and the coachman and middle-aged man did happen to be drinking ale with it. I worried about how tomorrow's drive would go, but giant tortoises were smart enough to drag us along fine, even if the coachman's whipping was haphazard.

I eventually got over my revulsion and ate the food like I would anything else. Next time I came to this town, though, I would probably go through this all over again. Lorraine said she wanted to come eat this again sometime, so we would likely stop by on the way home. I had to mentally prepare myself before then.

"Thanks to you two, we got to eat tasty food this whole trip! If we ever see you in Maalt, we'll treat you to something nice!" the young woman said after she got off the carriage.

"We owe you," her father added, standing next to her. "I heard you fought off some monsters one night, too. This isn't much, but here." He presented us with a bronze coin.

"No, we were only defending ourselves. If you want to do something for us, you can buy us a nice meal when you're back in Maalt, assuming you'll be back," Lorraine suggested.

We had talked to the middle-aged man and the young woman a fair bit, enough to know they were returning to the village where the woman's mother and grandparents lived. They stayed in Maalt for work most of the time but went back to their village when they had a vacation. The mother took care of the grandparents. It was a common story.

"Are you sure? Normally you'd pay a Silver-class adventurer in silver coins, even," the man said.

Silver-class and Bronze-class were convenient titles in that they provided an estimate of the price for the adventurer's services. Silver-class adventurers used to take one or two silver coins, but now they were even more expensive thanks to inflation. Bronze-class adventurers once took one bronze coin, but of course, their asking price had since increased as well. Still, we made one or two silver coins at the most. A Bronze-class adventurer's wallet was never in the best of states.

"It's fine. We weren't here on a job. It wasn't even out of the kindness of our hearts. We're traveling too, and it was nice to have people to talk to. See you later."

"Dang, you don't see a lot of generous adventurers nowadays. Fine, until next time, then," the middle-aged man said. He waved goodbye and entered the village with his daughter.

"Time to go," the coachman said and got the carriage moving. We were still on the third day of the journey. There were three or four more to go. The only passengers left were us, the coachman, and the old couple.

"I know I kept making fun of how rural your home is, but maybe I didn't go far enough," Lorraine said as she popped her head out of the carriage.

She was right. We were surrounded by nothing but mountains and forests. Up to where the father and daughter had disembarked, there were still roads like you would see around villages. But now there were mountains, mountains, mountains, forests, and more mountains. The road was leveled out enough that a carriage could cross it, but only just barely. The coachman had the skill, and the carriage had the durability to handle it, but this part was always scary. If the carriage broke down, we would have to walk.

The old couple had gotten off yesterday, by the way. The distance between the road and their destination would require them to walk a ways, so Lorraine and I had carried them the rest of the way there. Thankfully the coachman said he would wait for us to get back.

He even said he'd camp right there and wait for us to return if we didn't make it back that day. That was one nice advantage to country roads; the westbound carriages were never so flexible. They were often filled to capacity, and city folk were always concerned about getting to places on time. Late arrivals garnered tons of complaints, with passengers demanding their money back. On this road, no such thing was possible. That might have been partially because country people were lazier, but the coachman didn't expect to make much money no matter what happened, and the passengers were willing to go with the flow.

"Well, yeah, if it weren't so far out of the way, I'd visit home more often. It takes time to get here, time I didn't have. Thankfully now I can get by without working constantly, but I had to toil every day to put food on the table until recently," I said.

That was typical for Bronze-class adventurers. If you had a party, you could work more efficiently and avoid such poverty, but I didn't. Although, maybe I liked to waste money a little too much, too. I was obsessed with seemingly useless magic items.

"If you just told me you were going through rough times, I would've given you a loan with no interest."

"How could I ask for that? I want to be your equal."

I was afraid my destitution would leave me socially isolated too, but if Lorraine said she'd offer money, then she probably would. Even so, I didn't want to ask for some. Not while I still had other options, at least. If worse came to worst then I might have been forced to abandon my pride, but then I would strive to pay her back for the rest of my life. Long-time friends were precious to me.

"You don't need to be so stubborn. Well, maybe that's just how you are," she acknowledged.

It was true, I lived life how I wanted. If I gave that up, it would be the death of me. That's why, even though I was undead, I still thought of myself as alive. My will lived on.

The carriage continued onward for another half a day or so. "Almost there," the coachman muttered.

Lorraine and I looked outside and saw the road gradually becoming more open. We had reached the point where the road was used by the villagers of Hathara, so it was maintained to some degree. A river ran alongside the path, so that was probably why. I recognized the scenery around here.

"Finally," Lorraine said, exhausted. Even she had trouble with all the shaking. She was from the city, so I doubted she had ever ridden a carriage that rocked so much.

"I can see it now. It's the village of Hathara," I whispered.

Lorraine looked straight ahead too. "A wooden fence? Seems kind of primitive."

"It might look that way, but Hathara's medicine woman coats that fence in a drug that's extremely effective at warding off monsters. And if some monsters do get through, there are hunters that can take care of it. Their defenses are fine."

If anything too powerful appeared, they would have to call adventurers, but they had enough people who could take down goblins or slimes. Even deep in the mountains, life was possible.

"I already heard as much, but this village is a bit strange. There are autonomous cities with their own defenses against monsters, but not many small villages in the mountains can boast the same. Or maybe I'm just ignorant, and this is normal for mountain villages."

"I'm not sure. I used to think it was normal, but when I think about it now, it is kind of odd. The medicine woman's drugs are unusually effective, and the hunters seem stronger than they have any right to be."

"There's also that mysterious shrine where you were blessed. I told Hilde I was coming with you out of curiosity as an excuse, but it does sound interesting. I can't wait to investigate," Lorraine said with excitement.

I didn't mind, but to me, it was an ordinary village. I couldn't imagine she would find anything outside the shrine, but I could think about that after we got there. With that in mind, we waited for the carriage to reach the village.

Afterword

Thank you for reading *The Unwanted Undead Adventurer*, Volume 5. This is the author, Yu Okano. The fifth volume was published without a hitch, much to my relief. The light novels and the manga version are both ongoing, something I'm deeply thankful for.

But even after five volumes, I'm still worried about writing this afterword. I was never good at talking about myself, and even sitting here with my manuscript in front of me, I have no idea what to write. When it comes to novels, no matter how bad my writer's block gets, at least some sort of story will come out naturally once I sit down at my PC and write a few lines. It's just the afterwords that are a problem. I'll never get used to them.

Should I write about recent events in my life? I don't know if anyone cares about that. Should I write a behind-the-scenes story about this novel? I can't think of anything special to say. What if I wrote about my hobbies? I don't have much in the way of hobbies.

That's what runs through my head until, in the end, I write something worthless and call it a day. I'd like to write something more meaningful, but it's extremely difficult. I've checked to see what other authors write for reference, and they all have nice, genuine afterwords. They impress me, but I never get as far as figuring out what to do for my own afterwords, sadly.

Anyway, I thought this complaining would bring up my word count a decent amount, but I'm only about halfway to where I need to be. I have to write something more, but I can't think of anything. All that comes to mind is the aquarium in my room. One tiny hobby of mine is taking care of tropical fish. It used to just be tropical fish, but a lot of people have been obsessing over the layout of their aquatic plants lately, so I did the same thing. I have a fish tank with tropical fish and beautiful plants that's like a little garden. Just looking at it brings me peace. It feels like I'm creating my own small world, and that's kind of fun and exciting.

My novels are the same way. I set up characters, countries, and events to produce a whole world. Most of what occurs in that world is according to my intentions, but things have happened that I never expected when I started writing. That also applies to this afterword. I want to savor this work and the surprises that come with it, so that might be why I write novels. If I get to release another volume, maybe I'll write about those feelings in that afterword.

Anyway, I hope you'll continue to read *The Unwanted Undead Adventurer*. I have another novel coming out alongside this one called *The Middle-Aged Underdog Adventurer is Still Trying His Best*. If possible, I'd like it if you could give that a look too. That's all for now, see you next volume.

The Unwanted Undead Adventurer

NOVEL Volume 6: On Sale June 2022

THE
FARAWAY
PALADIN

The Archer of Beast Woods

Kanata Yanagino

lustrations by: Kususaga Rin

JOHN SINCLAIR ®

DEMON HUNTER

THE EUROHORROR LEGEND RETURNS!
AVAILABLE FROM ALL MAJOR
EBOOK STORES!

AUTHOR: JASON DARK

COVER ART: NAMCOOG

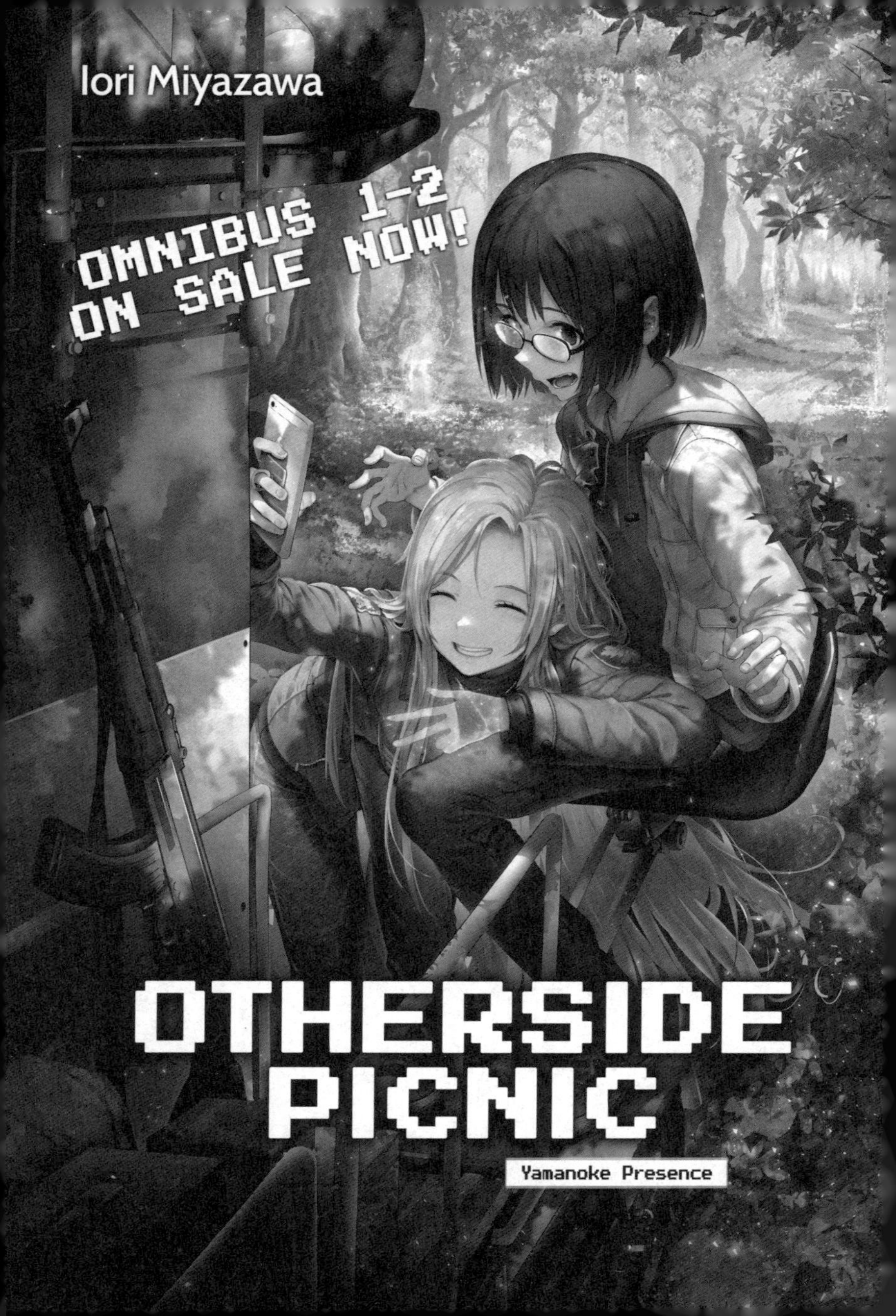
Iori Miyazawa
OMNIBUS 1-2
ON SALE NOW!
OTHERSIDE
PICNIC
Yamanoke Presence

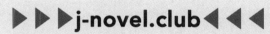

J-Novel Club Lineup

Latest Ebook Releases Series List

Altina the Sword Princess
Amagi Brilliant Park
Animeta!**
The Apothecary Diaries
An Archdemon's Dilemma:
  How to Love Your Elf Bride*
Are You Okay With a Slightly Older
  Girlfriend?
Arifureta: From Commonplace
  to World's Strongest
Arifureta Zero
Ascendance of a Bookworm*
Banner of the Stars
Bibliophile Princess*
Black Summoner*
The Bloodline
By the Grace of the Gods
Campfire Cooking in Another
  World with My Absurd Skill*
Can Someone Please Explain
  What's Going On?!
Chillin' in Another World with
  Level 2 Super Cheat Powers
The Combat Baker and Automaton
  Waitress
Cooking with Wild Game*
Culinary Chronicles of the Court
  Flower
Dahlia in Bloom: Crafting a Fresh
  Start with Magical Tools
Deathbound Duke's Daughter
Demon Lord, Retry!*
Der Werwolf: The Annals of Veight*
Dragon Daddy Diaries: A Girl
  Grows to Greatness
Dungeon Busters
The Emperor's Lady-in-Waiting Is
  Wanted as a Bride*
Endo and Kobayashi Live! The
  Latest on Tsundere Villainess
  Lieselotte
The Faraway Paladin*
Full Metal Panic!
Full Clearing Another World under
  a Goddess with Zero Believers*
Fushi no Kami: Rebuilding
  Civilization Starts With a Village
Goodbye Otherworld, See You
  Tomorrow
The Great Cleric
The Greatest Magicmaster's
  Retirement Plan

Girls Kingdom
Grimgar of Fantasy and Ash
Hell Mode
Her Majesty's Swarm
Holmes of Kyoto
How a Realist Hero Rebuilt the
  Kingdom*
How NOT to Summon a Demon
  Lord
I Shall Survive Using Potions!*
I'll Never Set Foot in That House
  Again!
The Ideal Sponger Life
If It's for My Daughter, I'd Even
  Defeat a Demon Lord
In Another World With My
  Smartphone
Infinite Dendrogram*
Invaders of the Rokujouma!?
Jessica Bannister
JK Haru is a Sex Worker in Another
  World
John Sinclair: Demon Hunter
A Late-Start Tamer's Laid-Back Life
Lazy Dungeon Master
A Lily Blooms in Another World
Maddrax
The Magic in this Other World is
  Too Far Behind!*
The Magician Who Rose From
  Failure
Mapping: The Trash-Tier Skill That
  Got Me Into a Top-Tier Party*
Marginal Operation**
The Master of Ragnarok & Blesser
  of Einherjar*
Min-Maxing My TRPG Build in
  Another World
Monster Tamer
My Daughter Left the Nest and
  Returned an S-Rank Adventurer
My Friend's Little Sister Has It
  In for Me!
My Instant Death Ability is So
  Overpowered, No One in This
  Other World Stands a Chance
  Against Me!*
My Next Life as a Villainess: All
  Routes Lead to Doom!
Otherside Picnic
Outbreak Company
Perry Rhodan NEO

Private Tutor to the Duke's
  Daughter
Reborn to Master the Blade: From
  Hero-King to Extraordinary
  Squire ♀*
Record of Wortenia War*
Reincarnated as the Piggy Duke:
  This Time I'm Gonna Tell Her
  How I Feel!
The Reincarnated Princess Spends
  Another Day Skipping Story
  Routes
Seirei Gensouki: Spirit Chronicles*
Sexiled: My Sexist Party Leader
  Kicked Me Out, So I Teamed U
  With a Mythical Sorceress!
She's the Cutest... But We're
  Just Friends!
The Sidekick Never Gets the Girl,
  Let Alone the Protag's Sister!
Slayers
The Sorcerer's Receptionist
Sorcerous Stabber Orphen*
Sweet Reincarnation**
The Tales of Marielle Clarac*
Tearmoon Empire
Teogonia
The Underdog of the Eight Great
  Tribes
The Unwanted Undead
  Adventurer*
Villainess: Reloaded! Blowing
  Away Bad Ends with
  Modern Weapons*
Welcome to Japan, Ms. Elf!*
The White Cat's Revenge as
  Plotted from the Dragon King'
  Lap
A Wild Last Boss Appeared!
The World's Least Interesting
  Master Swordsman

...and more!
* Novel and Manga Editions
** Manga Only
Keep an eye out at j-novel.club
  for further new title
  announcements!